Separate Ways

RELATIONSHIPS, DIVORCE & INDEPENDENCE OF MIND

Separate Ways

RELATIONSHIPS, DIVORCE & INDEPENDENCE OF MIND

VIRA HLADUN–GOLDMANN

Sweetpea
Press

NEW YORK, NEW YORK

Published by SWEETPEA PRESS
New York, NY 10022

Publisher's Cataloging-in-Publication Data
Hladun-Goldmann, Vira.
    Separate ways : relationships, divorce & independence
    of mind / Vira Hladun-Goldmann. — , 2002.
        p.   ;   cm.
        ISBN 0-9720578-0-3

    1. Divorce.   I. Title.

        2002   2002105442
    —dc21   CIP

06 05 04 03 02 ✦ 5 4 3 2 1

Project coordination by Jenkins Group, Inc. • www.bookpublishing.com

Printed in the United States of America

To My Parents
Supporting, loving, guiding,
What you gave me
Made me what I am

To My Darling Daughter
I hope I gave you what was given to me.
If I did,
soar.

ACKNOWLEDGMENTS

ELI, THANK YOU! I WOULD NOT HAVE WRITTEN this book without your support, cooperation and guidance. We had a wonderful time, didn't we? Tears, laughter and searching—digging down deep and coming up with wonderful memories, meaningful thoughts on which to ponder.

I will remember the special moments around the making of this book for a long time.

And, to Mr. and Mrs. Gottlieb, you have a wonderful son. You can be proud.

Until the next time . . .

— *Vira*

CONTENTS

ACKNOWLEDGMENTS vi

FOREWORD ix
by Judge Walter B. Tolub

INTRODUCTION 3

CHAPTER 1 7
The Three Phases of Life; The Importance of
Communication in Marriage

CHAPTER 2 21
The Good Divorce; Keeping a Marriage Diary; The
Importance of Separation

CHAPTER 3 31
Childhood; My Ukrainian-American Roots; Early
Life in Rochester, New York

CHAPTER 4 41
How to Find a Lawyer; Mediation Vs. Court; From
the Lawyers Point of View: Legal Impressions of a
Client Named Vira Goldmann

CHAPTER 5 59
Meeting and Marrying Robert; Discovering the
World of Business Together; The Nature of our
Partnership

CONTENTS

CHAPTER 6 75
The History of Divorce

CHAPTER 7 83
Going for 50%; The Process of Taking a Divorce
to Court

CHAPTER 8 91
Parents and Children: Installing a Strong Base
to Their Character; Mothers and Daughters;
My Work as a Teacher

CHAPTER 9 107
The Trial; The Importance of Preparation; Keeping
a Cool Head on the Stand

CHAPTER 10 119
The Role of Women in the World; Changing Social
Values; The Family Unit Under Siege

CHAPTER 11 129
The History of Women's Rights in America;
Getting the Vote; Women's Finances Today

CHAPTER 12 139
The Verdict

AFTERWORD 145

APPENDIX A 149
My Work Life

APPENDIX B 155
The Nuts and Bolts of How to Get a Divorce

APPENDIX C 163
Restoration and Me

APPENDIX D 169
Problem Solving in Life

APPENDIX E 175
Press Coverage of the Historic Event

FOREWORD

by Judge Walter B. Tolub,
Justice New York State Supreme Court

I'M THE JUDGE WHO TRIED THE GOLDMANN CASE, and I think one point on this case bears repeating up front. It is this: that in every one of the next three divorce cases I tried after ruling in the case of Goldmann vs. Goldmann, the lawyer representing the husband sooner or later got around to pointing to the wife and saying, "Mrs. X is no Vira Goldmann!"

That said, there was no particular momentous reason why this decision happened when it did. By this I mean that it didn't arrive as the end result of some larger social upheaval or trend. No, the law allowing me to give her 50 percent was already on the books. Mrs. Goldmann just presented her case very forcefully, with all the bona fides carefully laid out. She had it all there. She's a very charismatic individual, and her attorneys did a great job.

Up until the time of her trial there was a "glass ceiling," i.e. a figure of about 15 million dollars, beyond which, by tacit agreement among judges, equitable distribution no longer applied. Above that figure, judges and juries tended to rely on the English rule of law which runs, "give her enough to maintain the style to which she's grown accustomed." Clearly, the amount in this case was more than enough for that, but I decided in her favor in any case, shattering that glass ceiling of which I spoke. I should mention that the decision wasn't even especially difficult. Divorces with young children caught in the middle are the ones that cause anguish in a judge. The only anguish I had in this case was sifting through the mountain of paperwork her painstaking legal team had put together!

One of the things that impressed me in this case, aside from the state of preparation of Vira and her lawyers, was that the business associates of Robert Goldmann were deferential on the stand both to him AND her. They were often called as what are known as "hostile witnesses," i.e. witnesses to bolster Mr. Goldmann's case. But they were anything but hostile to Mrs. Goldmann. This, to me, was a clear if implicit sign of her worth. It was obvious she had established herself among his business people as someone to be reckoned with, and this was an important factor in convincing me of her value in the marriage.

In addition to this, I was presented with a number of magazine articles published during the years of their marriage, usually dealing with her antique collecting and restoration of houses, which clearly represented them as partners, as members of a team.

Then, of course, there was Vira herself. As a judge, you

learn to watch witnesses carefully, and I have to say that Vira was a model. She was an independent, strong-willed, no-nonsense person who came across as a businesswoman—fully the equal of her husband.

In *matrimonials*, as these cases are known, there is often a lot of name-calling, with lawyers playing off the bitterness by filing motions—a process which doesn't exactly hurt these lawyer's incomes, by the way. I was struck by the fact that in this case there was no name-calling, and no bitterness either. In fact, unless I'm mistaken, there was actually some affection in the air.

Vira had always cut Robert's hair, despite him at a certain point becoming a very wealthy man. And this became a catch phrase or shorthand for a woman's full participation in a marriage. And Vira herself, thereby, became the model of a woman who should share fully in the fruits of that marriage.

As to advice for women entering a divorce court, I have several thoughts on the matter. First, the burden is on a woman—if she is not the breadwinner—to show concretely how she contributed to the marriage. A documentation of that contribution is important, but as a judge I can tell you right now: don't give me a daily log. Demonstrate that you went to 400 dinners, that you entertained his clients, etc., but don't give me the menus and the invitations. Show that you worked, that you contributed, even if indirectly. Marrying someone and staying at home popping bon-bons is not going to win you a judge's favor if the marriage comes apart. I've known hat check girls who married millionaires and thought of "work" as the time spent carrying the Tiffany's bag from the store to the waiting limo.

No, you must be realistic about your large-scale contribution, but don't exaggerate and don't embroider. If you do, you'll turn the judge off. Be specific. If you really believe you made a contribution, then make it concrete.

Oh, and by the way: I'm out of matrimonials as of April 2000. My blood pressure is already down ten points!

Separate Ways

RELATIONSHIPS, DIVORCE & INDEPENDENCE OF MIND

INTRODUCTION

MY DIVORCE WAS THE SINGLE MOST CHALLENGING and interesting experience so far in my life. I enjoyed crafting the case with the lawyers, and I was educated and entertained by the trial itself. My purpose in writing this book is to give women facing the end of a marital relationship the two things they need most: information and confidence. Confidence springs directly FROM information. And with confidence comes that little lever with which you can move mountains, which becomes strength, which then gives self-esteem.

When I lectured on relationships and divorce, one of the things that struck me most was the lack of knowledge and preparation that women so often seemed to have at this crucial crossroads in their lives. Here they were, about to embark on a trip into the American legal system that would have profound effects on their future on every level, and they seemed utterly unprepared. They were without a real strategy, and had no concept what to do to bring the situation to a victorious close. Often, though they themselves had instigated the divorce process, they were too caught up with their own turbulent emotional state to think clearly and muster the strength necessary for the challenges awaiting them. More often than not, they were having trouble finding a lawyer who would represent their interests intelligently and sympathetically.

In a situation like this, with the cards—financial, legal and emotional—stacked so hugely against her, how could a woman do anything but begin to fall apart? Confused and disoriented, she would present herself in a position of maximum vulnerability, leaving herself open to be taken advantage of. And once a climate of defeat is established around a woman seeking divorce, the end is more or less pre-ordained: she will be dealt with unfairly by both her husband and the legal system generally and end up with an enormous, often life-long burden on her shoulders.

In writing this book, I've wanted to share my own case and life in some detail—to open myself to the reader so that she may, in the old phrase, "see me plain." My divorce shattered precedents in the legal world, but in MY world, it was merely another chapter in the ongoing book of my life. I went into it with confidence, and I had no doubts from the start that I was going to get exactly what I deserved.

First myth to be disposed of: divorce is a negative. Really? I don't think so! The word I'm looking for is "freedom," as in, "not having to answer to anyone but myself." I earned my freedom in 10,000 days of cutting his hair and dressing him in clothes, and I earned it in cooking and serving his dinner for thirty-three years. I earned my "just desserts" in cleaning, organizing, furnishing, and running a house; in raising our daughter to be a wonderful woman; in advising, counseling, and troubleshooting for my husband: in being his lover, his best friend, his sounding board, his mother, and his sister, too.

Many people are frightened by divorce and frightened by the sight of a woman taking her destiny into her own hands. For those people I have a simple message: get used to it! I don't find my divorce unusual in any way. The numbers may have been larger, but the principles were exactly the same. Mine was simply a clear-headed response to a difficult situation.

Notice that phrase "clear-headed." Any woman seeking a divorce must first get down to the bare bones of who she is. She must know the answers to the questions: Who am I and what was I in this marriage?

Some real emotional and analytic work is necessary—digging down deep, pulling your inner self out and standing her up in front of you, eyeball to eyeball. You must look at yourself straight on, face to face, and see the negatives and positives. This is best done with a notebook in hand, thinking back over the landscape of the marriage, noting details and the daily contributions you made that helped keep it a loving, safe, and productive nest. The advantage of writing down the History of Your Marriage is twofold: it can have a crucial use in making your case later on, and in the meantime, it encourages you to make connections you wouldn't otherwise. One thing flows from another, and you begin to grow and evolve in your self-awareness. You start to see very clearly who you were, who you are and who, most of all, you're going to be. Women often worry: I'm getting a divorce; I'll be alone. Well, once you've gone through the process of self-searching, you won't worry. Why? Because you'll have an ampler sense of who you are and where you're going.

Noting this kind of information down is also useful for how it offsets the way in which married women, and especially women in long marriages, tend to take so much for granted. They say, "It's silly; I got up every morning for ten years and put cereal in the bowl for Tom and Mary and the Big Guy. What kind of contribution is that?" The correct answer is: a big one. If you hadn't done those things, the family would have gone out the door discombobulated and hungry and performed sub-par for the day. Little overlooked things like these eventually add up to a large—actually critical—contributions in the larger mosaic of family and home.

Once this information is gathered, you're then ready to create a team: yourself and the particular lawyer or mediator who will work well with you and BELIEVE IN YOU. And you've got to prepare this all in advance, too. You can't go in cold. If you go in cold, and you're an emotional wreck to boot, forget it; you've lost before you started. You've got to go in with a strong first step—confident, informed, knowing exactly where you want to go.

If you're holding this book in your hands, you are about to embark on a new life.

CHAPTER

1

The Three Phases of Life;
The Importance of
Communication in Marriage

CHAPTER 1

I NEVER DREAMED OF MARRIAGE AS MANY OF MY friends did. For them, marriage was above all a beautiful storybook ceremony, with yards of white lace, tossed rice, and crying relatives. To me, marriage as a girl meant partnership, because that was how my parents lived. Perhaps I'm unusual, but for me "holy matrimony" was merely another challenge in the ongoing work of my life. A big challenge, perhaps, and along with the birth of my daughter Olexa, one of the central projects of my life, but something which, after the dust of romance had settled, I had to work at, slowly and even methodically. I hesitate to call it a job, marriage, especially given how associated it is with myths of eternal happiness, but there are ways in which it is that, with all the routine, the work, and the sacrifice that a job entails. The upside, of course, is the way in which, like fine wine, a long relationship can lead to an exquisite mellowing over the years.

But let us remember that not all old wine mellows. It can also, without any warning, turn to vinegar in the bottle.

I've always believed there are three phases in a life. The first is birth and growing and developing, during which you learn who you are and what you're going to attempt to achieve with your life. The second is the period of that achievement, during which you do more or less what society expects of you: developing your skills, raising a family, maturing in your career. The third phase is the one in which you've satisfied all the outer requirements in life and can look toward the future while listening only to your own inner promptings. The third phase is for yourself.

In this third phase, you've been polished by life to a gleam. You're not the spring chicken anymore but the old hen in the barnyard, become wiser as result of all those hard knocks and experiences in the life you've had up until then. You're seasoned and experienced; you've done your homework, been a good student all those years, and it's time to graduate from worrying about the outer world of others to the world of yourself. You are free; you've become a soul unhooked from all the grinding responsibilities. This is your life; you can do what you please. You are often ready, if need be during this third phase, to go it alone.

Sometime during our twenty-fifth year of marriage, I remember turning to my husband, Robert, and saying, "Robert, the first twenty-five were yours, the next twenty-five will be mine." He gave me his standard vague smile and seemed not to take any real notice. After twenty-five years of having me as his caretaker, how could he possibly think anything would change?

But I had begun listening to that inner voice, and change is exactly what I was determined to make happen.

The truth of the matter is that over time, we'd simply grown apart. The writer Anton Chekov says somewhere, "if you fear loneliness, don't get married." What he meant, I think, is that in a long-term marriage, a kind of auto-pilot mentality can take over at a certain point, replacing the pleasure of togetherness with a slightly robotic daily life. A lot of this is a result of a simple medical fact: we are now living longer than in the past, and the chance of staying with a mate for thirty, forty, or fifty years is increasingly possible. One is constantly changing, mutating, and developing. That process never stops. So in a long-term marriage, one is faced with the alternative of either actively working at following one another through the various changes, partnering one another over time as if in a dance, or hardening in each respective position and growing apart. The latter is what happened to us. Robert seemed to contract in his sixties, to withdraw from the surface of a life I felt myself wanting to rush out and embrace. I began to open up in late-middle age. I've always been a late bloomer, and so, as I say, I began to bloom.

The differences in my and Robert's outlooks became increasingly clear in discussions of our future. I've always been a future-oriented person. Perhaps it's a result of growing up with such pragmatic parents, but my whole life long I've kept a weather eye peeled on what the future would bring. It was the same in our marriage. Robert, in fact, used to kiddingly call me, "The Five-Year Plan." And once we'd arrived at that late-middle-aged phase of things, with our daughter out of the house and me, in a certain sense, "retired" from motherhood, I began to think clearly and calmly about "What Next."

For several years, in fact, I had been "seeding" our daily conversations with thoughts about what we might do in our "golden years." And yet, Robert simply and categorically refused to discuss it with me. Under no circumstances would he talk to me about the future except in the blandest most general terms. On business matters, he was a fountain of conversation. But on things to do with our future post-retirement, I might as well have been talking to an empty chair.

One of the main things I wanted to do at this crucial point in life was start a foundation—to give something back. Growing up as I did amidst modest means, I felt a deep indebtedness to this country which had been so generous to my parents and me. Also, for inspiration, there was the example of my father who believed money was really only useful for how it could help others. He was one of the executors of the Ukrainian Congress Committee, and after the second World War, he sponsored 200 immigrants to come to the states, found jobs for them, places to stay, and a way to get started in their new American lives.

From the beginning, it made little sense to me to simply accumulate money for the purpose of letting it lie around gathering interest. I loved the adventure and education of collecting fine art, antiques, and eighteenth-century structures, but I also had a real driving desire to put the money to use to uphold the principles I believed in.

So, at a certain point, I went to Robert with my thoughts on what I hoped would be called "The Robert and Vira Goldmann Foundation." I was so excited by this that even though I could tell Robert wasn't that interested, I forced a meeting on him with a foundation specialist. To indulge me, he went along. And after that, he confirmed my worst suspicions: he did nothing at all and actively discouraged me in my attempts to raise the subject.

I think I even know why. To him, it was all part of the deep and anguishing question: what to do after retirement? I used to ask myself, "Does this man think he's going to take it with him?" As intelligent and successful as he was, why couldn't he understand that life would not continue as it always was, but that it would change, that he would age and eventually die? But he couldn't get it. He had no consuming hobbies, no energizing passions. His business was his baby and his entire world. Robert, over time, had become a businessman down to his fingernails. He was a loving father and a fundamentally decent and kind human being, but he was also someone who proceeded down a single track in life like a train, without looking to either side.

Whenever I brought up issues of the future, and of perhaps thinking of changing our approach to life—opening ourselves up to something other than our routine—I received the very same response: he would get grim, set his mouth, and then announce, "I'm tired" and go to bed. He had a reflex reaction of shut-down whenever I attempted to make him confront the future. In contrast to Robert, I was and am a born communicator, a person who verbalizes, discusses, and analyzes things to death.

The Importance of Communication In a Marriage

I understood what was going on but seemed unable to reach him, despite my communication skills. It was almost as if he wanted to postpone the future entirely. I had already introduced him to travel, with the thought that we might eventually, upon retirement, live elsewhere part of the time. But though I tried everything I could to stimulate, motivate, cajole, and bring reality to him, he turned a deaf ear.

In truth, I think he was terrified.

I've thought about all these issues a lot, searched for reasons for his absolutely watertight denial of the future, and have come to realize something. I think Robert knew, deep down, the way an animal knows, that he was simply not going to live that long a time on this earth. I can't help but think that he knew he was going to die.

His body had begun to give off signals several years earlier. In his late fifties, he lost a lot of weight for no known reason. Then, increasingly, he became forgetful and absent-minded. Incidents began to happen. Like most men I've ever met, he insisted on driving the car at all times, even when tired. This I could cope with. What I had a little more difficulty with was when he began doing things like making left-hand turns from the far-right lane. The first time I saw this, I thought: my goodness, what's wrong with him? Another time we were in the Hamptons, coming back from Montauk, and he nearly hit a pair of joggers—an accident averted at the last minute by me shouting a warning at him, though of course, he pretended that he'd known all along, and it was "under control."

The straw that broke the camel's back took place while we were on our way to in-laws in California one day. We were on a residential road, as I recall, and we came upon a sign mentioning that Route 100 could be accessed by the left lane. Now, Robert always loathed back seat drivers, and over time I had grown habituated to not criticizing his increasingly distracted driving habits. This particular time, he moved across the left lane and all the way into the oncoming traffic lane. I saw what he'd done, but I said to myself, "I'm not going to say anything." Robert didn't want a backseat driver? OK, I surreptitiously put my foot near the brake and my hand near the door, prepared to bail out before the impact. Lo and behold, as we approached a sharp turn in the road, a huge group of cyclists suddenly appeared. Robert seemed to awaken from his trance, and with his reflexes still working, he swung the car back into the proper lane. As we continued on from our near tragedy, I idly pointed out landmarks and how lovely and green the California hills were, and I pretended as if nothing had happened.

When we finally arrived at our hotel in Santa Barbara, the valet took our car, and as Robert was walking with me to the front desk, he said, "I think we'll take a plane back to Los Angeles."

"Good idea," I said, and that was the last time I ever got into a car with him.

What it was at bottom was a kind of circulatory insufficiency: the blood was not getting to the brain. The result of this was a series of tiny strokes—mini blackouts so quick that I didn't realize they were even happening. Robert stonewalled my inquiries into his health like a trained witness facing hostile cross-examination. When he collapsed one day in the bathroom and came to on his own, I didn't find out until he mentioned it casually while we were out with another couple!

Another day he had to leave for a board meeting, early in the morning, and woke me up by saying matter of factly, "I can't lift my arm up." The next afternoon, he went to a doctor.

I told him to remind the doctor about the symptoms of the day before, and he blew up at me with annoyance, saying, "Don't make me out to be an old man!"

He kept his medical reports private and blocked every attempt for me to intervene and get him into a cardiac or circulatory program of some sort. Part of it was that he saw me as very youthful, energetic, and still ambitious, and saw himself slowing down, and resented it, and was frightened by it. I, for my part, was growing increasingly angry and frustrated at what I saw as his inability to respond, to open or change to accommodate the changes that were taking place with both him and me.

In the meantime, during the last year of our marriage, there had been a series of events that had precipitated a crisis. Part of this crisis was due to him presenting me with a series of financial documents that I found very demeaning for how they reduced me to the role of a child in deciding my own destiny and tossed thirty-five years of my competence as wife, mother, and businesswoman out the window. That didn't help the climate, I can tell you!

Yet, despite all this, despite the fact that we were on that auto-pilot which can happen to long-married couples, I still had hopes of there being some kind of a breakthrough. I realized I was reaching the point of no return, but I still wanted to give him one last chance. After all, affection dies hard, as does the habit of togetherness.

As I recall, I was washing the dishes after dinner one night around this time, and while doing so, said with a calmness that belied the intensity behind my question, "Robert, you really must talk to me here. I mean, what do you want to do?

Do you think not facing the future means the future won't happen? What on God's earth do you want to do when you sell the company?"

I'll never forget the ways his eyes went beady and small, and his mouth clenched tight, and a terrible terrible flare of violent hostility went through the room. There was a long, seemingly endless silence. At that moment I said to myself: it's clear what my position is in this relationship. It was also clear to me at that very same moment that we were no longer a team.

Premonitions

Actually, for awhile I had had the strangest sensation around Robert, a sensation that had made me want to flee. For the entire last year of our marriage, I began to feel and see death around him. I used to close my eyes and see a black hole in the garden. And that was my grave, and if I would stay on with him, I would enter that black hole. He would be taking me to the grave with him. I would see it when I would shut my eyes or when I would think about it.

It was like a white aura or a cloud around him, this strange specter of death. I remember I was in the foyer of our home one day about this time, and I had opened the door to step out into the narrow hallway, and he passed by me and never saw me, nose to nose; he just drifted by. It was like he was sleepwalking—not entirely in his body. And I saw a distinct white cloud around him. It was as if he were already, partially, somewhere else.

I began to feel this sense of impending death around me. It was strange, yes, but not at bottom that disturbing. I've always been mediumistic, highly attuned to the spiritual in life, and I took this all as an affirmation that it was time for me to go. And then the strangest thing happened.

I was at a luncheon function one day, during the period in which Robert and I had agreed on a separation, and he was planning to move out shortly. I was seated at this function next to a young woman whom I had never met before. We were having one of those casual, getting-to-know-you kind of conversations, when she asked me where I lived. In a general way I said I used to live on Park Avenue but had since moved. And she asked, "Well tell me, does your husband live there with you?"

Well, yes, I said, looking at her a little strangely, and then laughing, told her, yes, but only for three more weeks.

I'm so sorry, she said, but when you came up to the table, I saw a black aura around you, and I saw a black hole next to it. I couldn't help but mention it to you.

Don't apologize, I said, let me tell you about that black hole. That's the black hole that I see in my garden. And if I stay married to him, I will walk out into that garden and lay down inside that black hole. The woman nodded, as if understanding everything.

As I say, we had decided finally on a separation, and set a date for him to move out. It was the culmination of a years-long phase of gradual, growing estrangement. I still recall the final scene of my thirty-three-year marriage. As such things often do, it ended unsentimentally and entirely dry-eyed. He came upstairs to say goodbye. And I said, don't say goodbye; just say so-long. Goodbye, to me, was far too permanent. So long meant that we would still continue friendly dialogue. Take good care of yourself, dear, I added. And then he left. And as he left the house, death walked right out the door with him.

18

I was enormously relieved. It was over at last! This was the beginning of my new life, and I felt free. For several years, whenever I traveled and was flying in the sunny space up above the clouds, I would look out the window, and I would see a wonderful, statuesque bird sitting out on the edge of those clouds, and that bird was me, And when he moved out I was free, I could fly anywhere I wanted to fly; I was exuberant and champing at the bit to start a new life. And I felt sorry for him because he didn't have what I had, and he should have. After so many years of struggling and working to succeed, now was the time for a change, a new life, and he couldn't see that and never would. I was sad for him, that he never had that last part of his life—that third act—which can be so full of rich experiences that bring life to its fullest satisfaction. He only opened the door to the third part of his life and never went through it.

CHAPTER

2

*The Good Divorce,
Keeping a Marriage Diary;
The Importance of Separation*

CHAPTER 2

NO TWO MARRIAGES ARE ALIKE, BUT ALL MARRIAGES when they're coming to an end finish in the same way: divorce. My contention is that this event, which is traditionally associated with the saddest, most tragic side of life, is anything but. It's freedom and light from where I'm standing. All women facing divorce have a period ahead of them not only of challenge but of real possibility for growth. Positive growth. That's right, there is such a thing as a successful divorce, just as there is such a thing as a good divorce. Though people are unused to seeing those words together, I hope they become more commonly linked in the future. A successful divorce is a divorce that is concluded quickly, fairly, and with a just distribution of the marital assets. A good divorce is a divorce that allows a woman to drop old destructive habits and open herself toward a future bright with new potential.

A divorcing woman has an opportunity for once to be "self" centered in the best sense of that word. After a divorce, a woman begins doing things with a new respect for her own time and space. Women in these circumstances begin to write. They paint. They begin to enrich themselves in their own home. They heal. It's the beginning of privileging the "you" part of yourself, carving it out of your schedule. A woman has to be ready, of course. A lot of this begins with the process of listening to oneself. A lot of people don't listen to themselves, but a divorcing or just divorced woman should have her ear cocked and ready at all hours. She should ask herself: Where are am I mentally? Where am I emotionally? What is the trail of breadcrumbs that brought me to this pass, and where do I want to be a year from now? She has not only to talk to herself but listen as well. Don't take yourself for granted. Don't demean yourself. Realize your competence in having raised children or run a home. You have to look yourself straight in the eye, look at the pros and the cons of yourself as clearly as you can, and decide what you want to keep and what to try to discard. Divorce offers the chance for that kind of thought process. And then you go from there.

Which brings me to the heart of my advice on what to do to help yourself at this crucial juncture of your life: the History of My Marriage. When you realize that your own marriage may end in divorce, one of the things you must set yourself to do as soon as possible is to begin to keep a diary dedicated to showing what it is you do in a typical married day. Unsure of your importance to the family nest? Write down everything you did to help the family that day, and you'll understand the importance of your role, loud and clear. Just make a list of every single thing. Then go to the next day. And I mean every single thing. Let's say you wake up in the morning with three children and a husband. Breakfast is a major event—a hundred details you run together to make it go smoothly. You write that down. Did you pack them a lunch? Write that down. Today we went to the zoo and saw the African Habitat. Write that down. Did your daughter get an A on the paper that you worked with her on last night? Did your son win the spelling bee? Did you spend time with your kindergarten-age kids and drill them on what the rock does and what the leaf does? Did you walk them down the driveway to the street to the school bus? Write all of it, in all its detail, down on the page.

If a woman running a family doesn't have outside help, then she does all that and also the dishes, the laundry, the mopping, the sewing, the gardening, the dusting, and the washing-up. It's all invisible to the wider world, and it's all as important as vitamins and minerals to the health of a family. Rack 'em up, and write 'em down!

Here is a woman sitting in the middle of her busy day: kids at school, a thousand things to do, and yet she creates that hour of space for herself and she writes in a book she's bought just for the purpose, which she's entitled, "The History of My Marriage." Why is she writing the list of what she's contributed to her loving nest? So she can realize what she has given to the partnership, for one. But also, and more importantly, so that she can begin the process of recognizing her value. Because she takes herself for granted. She can't help herself. She along with everybody else on the planet does a variety of small things a day to benefit her near and dear that she doesn't even think of and pays no attention to. This could range from teaching a two-year-old to brush her teeth, to shoveling snow off the walk.

But she is not only keeping a daily graph of her marriage and the hundred small things she is doing to sustain it. She is also going back in time, to the beginning of her marriage. She is going through her sadness to grasp the origins of her relationship, and to write of what she did for her family—that is the key: what she did to help build the family, from the very first day she married.

From this diary, our writer will begin sorting out the information, and patterns will emerge. A growing sense of self-recognition will accrue. And many months later, when and if she seeks out lawyers, this History of My Marriage will be a crucial blueprint for getting a fair share of the marital assets. In the meantime, however, it will be a lifeline of clarity for a woman in the rocky moment of a bad marriage, a tool to allow herself to pull herself up by the bootstraps, and for that, an invaluable resource in a time of trial.

The Importance of Separation

During this period, this phase of marriage-ending, a woman is prey to flaring emotions. There's really nothing to be done about it, and it comes with the territory. Yet the fruit of my experience can be boiled down to this: try not to let yourself become a hostage to your feelings. Try not to let your emotions become a sled that carries you away to a place you don't want to go. Not only because it's bad for you personally and psychologically, but because when you enter the arena of a divorce, you enter a legal process that will be carried out according to precise—sometimes obscure—rules. Nothing will be gained by you being emotionally and mentally bogged down.

My advice, therefore, is simple: if you feel you're in such a state, you should let some time go. Achieve a separation.

A waiting period can be the perfect thing to calm the nerves and give you needed clarity. Take some time for yourself during this separation. Catch up on things you've neglected in the hullabaloo of finding that your marriage was concluding. Often this phase takes a year. It usually begins with one of the two moving out. The truth of the matter is that once this point has been reached, there is no turning back. That's why during the separation I would suggest that you not see each other any more than is necessary.

Backsliding is so easy that it's a form of human nature, really. When the clothes are still in the same closets, and the question can still be asked, "should we go out to dinner tonight?" you are not separated. You may be playing at separation, but you are not separated at all.

So take a year, and live apart. It will not be an easy year. It will be a year of slow, steady clarification. During this year you must "cut the cord." The point in all this is to bring about a state of closure, because it's only with closure that you can begin a new life. What you DON'T want to do, above all else, is fall into one of those states of limbo, a kind of low-wattage depression in which you're paralyzed and can watch entire years drift by in a state of inaction. No, this is a time for action, action, action above all!

Begin preparing the paperwork for divorce: gather the banking and legal documents, and the various financial instruments testifying to your shared holdings. Make copies and keep them in a safe place. And another thing: don't be shy. You're getting a divorce, not a murder rap. Sometimes—as in trying to kick cigarettes—going public with your intentions makes it easier to follow-through.

For myself, I'd have taken out an ad in the *New York Times* if I'd have thought of it.

Once you've decided to get a divorce, and have gone public with it, you will discover that divorce is a kind of social truth test, which will reveal to you who your true friends are. Don't be hurt by the fact that divorce polarizes the people around the divorcing couple. Expect it, if anything. For a variety of reasons, many old friends will stop calling. They'll feel jealousy, and they'll also be a bit uncomfortable at the way in which a divorce forces them to take a good hard look at their own marriages. Without intending to, you'll have become a bit of a stirrer-upper. Half the people you know are probably less than happy with their marriage, and so your action acts as an irritant of a sort, and for those people who can't face the truth, well, that's the end of what may be, for you, a treasured relationship.

Then there's the Great Gulf situation. Often people feel they have to side with one or the other, Him or Her. They make their decision accordingly. In the long run, anyone who would turn on you in such a situation is someone you wouldn't want anything to do with. And remember: a divorce is not a closing-down so much as an opening up. So whatever friends fall by the wayside will be replaced by new people who will suit your new life.

Yes, in the aftermath of a divorce, there is a void, but that void can also be pleasurable, because an unnatural situation has resolved itself, and there is a sense of new access and new possibility. In my case there was no sadness. It was the threshold of my new life. The caterpillar had become the butterfly, leaving her cocoon behind. I was sitting at the edge of my own life, waiting to take off, and finally, with a flutter of wings, I did.

CHAPTER

3

Childhood;
My Ukrainian-American Roots;
Early Life in Rochester, New York

CHAPTER 3

THE FOUNDATION FOR THIS THIRD AND FULFILLING stage of my life was established in the first part of my life—my beginnings. I'm descended on both sides from hard-working Ukrainians, and their strong ethical sense and honest principles have shaped my life. My father was born in a small village called Cerche, in Ukraine, where he came from a family of landowners who endowed him with pride, curiosity and a methodical nature. My mother came from a very poor peasant village, born into a family that worked the fields. From the first, my mother was a hard worker, as was her mother before her.

Ukrainian women work. This is not a pampered species. They work alongside the men in the fields, pulling their weight. And when they come to a foreign country, they do the same thing. In the peasant villages, you would always see the labor equally distributed, whether it be hoeing, milking, bringing in the crops, or cooking the food. And the same held true in my own family.

I was born in Rochester, New York, a cold industrial town about two hours south of the Canadian border, made famous by local son George Eastman, who had founded Kodak. We lived in an immigrant neighborhood of clean but dreary clapboard row-houses. The Polish section was at one end, the Jewish at another, and between them was a mixed salad of ethnicities: German, Italian, and others.

These people, like most American immigrants, were hardworking, thrifty, and diligent. They worked on cars, they cooked in restaurants, they were employed on assembly lines in factories, or like my father, they managed the Dollar Dry Cleaning company, or like my mother, tailored clothes. It was a blue collar area, and yet it was immaculate. These people were proud of their lives and their new adventure in America. They scrubbed and drained and cleaned, and the neighborhood shone like a jewel.

Our home was a tiny dot of a place, in the classic proletarian row-house style, with lace curtains, small front and rear porches, and a perfect tiny garden in which my mother spent some of her happiest times. Inside the house, our lives revolved around the kitchen. I clearly recall the sunny space, with its bright speckled linoleum floor, and its beautiful metal art-deco table, upon which my mother heaped that great conversational motivator: food. Around this table, we only spoke Ukrainian at first. Ukrainian, spoken properly, is a language of great warmth and heart, perfectly adapted to the home. But partly because my father was desirous of entering American life to the fullest, he refused to live in an exclusively Ukrainian neighborhood. Therefore it was driven home to me from the beginning that we were different from other people, that not everyone ate borscht, varenyky, or the hearty warm black bread of the Ukraine.

"Don't eat American bread," my mother would say, frowning at the brightly colored package of Wonderbread. "It's like eating baked air."

When I look back at myself, I see a lively, imaginative girl, her hair in pigtails, dressed in a jumper sewn for her by her mother, who was deeply attached to her parents, and lived in a tiny bedroom that gave out onto the street. The street—this is before the days of asphalt—was made of Belgian paving stones, and if I woke up early enough, I was rewarded with the sights and sounds of the horse-drawn milkwagon or ice truck clopping peacefully past our house. I was always fascinated by the behavior of the horses themselves—old bow-necked veterans who would know instinctively when to stop and when to start again without being told.

The ice-man carried a veritable berg on the back of his wagon, and it was a miracle to me that he always knew just how to tap with his pick so that a perfectly shaped slab of ice slid off—ice that he then heaved onto his back and carried into our house to keep our perishables fresh another week. We kids would run behind his wagon and scavenge for chips to keep cool in the heat.

The house inside was frugally furnished but warm with life. Windows let in the light on a large, open first-floor space which, with its double hurricane lamps, its doilies, piano, bookshelf, desks, and comfortable reading chair for my father, was decorated in deeply American style. But draped on the piano was a bright, embroidered towel, made for my father by his sisters, and symbolizing to me the far-away place from which my parents had come—the mysterious, exotic land of Ukraine.

Children live happily in their fantasy worlds, and I was no different. In our small home I constructed an entire universe of tiny play environments. The dark yet cozy stone basement, blackened in one corner from the coal bin, was where my mother washed the clothes and where I set up my grocery store. I had a miniscule cash register and my make-believe friends would come by to shop. Since my mother did a lot of canning every fall with fruits and vegetables gathered from her garden, I had a constant stock of pickles, tomatoes and peaches and pears to sell and buy. In the library upstairs where my fathers kept his books, I had my own mini-library, where I lent out books and fined late borrowers. The attic was another treasure trove, filled with the comforting smell of old wooden beams, and piled with endless swatches and rolls of fabric, needles and thread, and all the other paraphernalia of sewing. My mother was a pack-rat before the word was even invented. She never threw anything away.

Rochester, New York, was, as I said, the town that George Eastman, the founder of Kodak, built. He endowed a variety of local institutions, but more to the point, nearly every citizen had a Brownie camera as a point of pride.

Our attic was jammed with photographs of my parents in their youth in Ukraine: dressed with pride in their best clothes, though they had no money at all; and of the relatives looking out at the camera with their stern, strong-boned faces. Despite their poverty, my family was always attracted to clothes. In the

36

Ukraine, some of the men dressed as dandies, in knee-high leather boots and the sporty caps of the period.

One of my favorite things to do was to pose the older Ukrainian photos of my parents against those taken of them after they'd arrived in American and become "modern." So, next to the older photo of my father—handsome, brooding, with heavy-lidded eyes and full lips, in his captains fur-lined uniform of the Ukrainian Army and boots or in an Edwardian cream-colored linen suit and cane, I would place a photo of his Americanized self—wearing a snappy suit and Brylcreemed hair, posing rakishly against a 1934 Reo. I would put the photo of my mother, in her traditional village costume of heavy embroidered linen with wool vests, next to a photo taken just a few years later, in which, having made her way to the States, she wore a fancy new American hair-do, daring off-the-shoulder straps (made and designed by her), and a dashing string of pearls.

Both of my parents were beautiful, well-groomed people on whom clothes hung with the natural fall of clothes on a model. For this reason, while they were courting amidst the lilacs in nearby Highland Park, they were constantly inter-rupted by photographers who wanted to pose them!

I would often go up to the attic to browse amidst these romantic images while clutching Butch, the light of my life, a little green handmade woolen dog, without whom I couldn't sleep at night.

We were a family unit, emotional and argumentative as many immigrant families are, and tightly linked one to anoth-er. We cooked together, we ate together, and at night, my bed-time stories were all from the old country: about the hardships of childhood in the Ukrainian village, the incredible superstitions, the great snows that crunched underfoot; and how when my mother cut herself a deep gash climbing a fence and ran home bleeding, her grandmother, who was doing the wash, took one look at her and simply plunged the whole hand into a boiling wash vat; how she slept on straw spread behind the oven for warmth, and how she protected her thick-witted sister who was too slow to learn how to guide the horses for plowing. She laughed as she explained that their father finally grew so exasperated with her sister that he instructed her by sitting in a chair behind her, angrily yanking one pigtail as he shouted "Right!" and another for "Left!" I would kiss them good night, and then my father would say, "Luba turn that light off!" I would look upwards to the twirling porcelain ballerina lamp over my bed as I snapped out the light. I used to think she was the prettiest dancer in the world.

Everything we did was *en famille*, including weekend trips to the Sun Theatre—an old, disinfectant-smelling place run by an Italian family that gave dishes away as door prizes. There we sat in the dark while flickering newsreels depicted ominous stirrings in Europe. We watched amazed at the exploits of Tarzan. The three of us all loved John Hodjak, the Ukrainian-American actor, as well as that other famous Ukrainian-American, Jack Palance. At home, on the radio, it was Jack Benny who made my parents laugh the hardest.

But these happy entertainments paled next to my father's interest in education and culture. *These* were the serious things of life, not the fluff and nonsense of radio comedians and movie stars. What he delighted in was the cut and thrust of political debate, animated discussions of current events, and debates on history and the future of Ukraine, which he had on a nearly weekly basis with Mr. Shelchik, the butcher. It was he who, after much serious thought, chose the local elementary school (kindergarten) for me. And that was where the problems began.

It was in kindergarten that I realized I wasn't like the rest of the kids. I still remember looking around, thinking, "Who *are* all these people?" In nursery school, I'd been merely unhappy, feeling cast out from the warmth of the familial nest. At five I realized I was actually different. Where other people said milk, I knew the liquid to be "moloko." Where other people said egg, I said "yaytsya." I was the only child in the classroom with immigrant parents, and this was a subtle but very real weight to carry around. There's an innate confidence that children have whose parents were born in that country and whose very first words are in the same language they will later encounter in school. My English, at the beginning, was spotty, and I suffered from insecurity as a result. Yet these difficulties helped form my character and instilled some backbone in me at an early age. I learned pretty quickly that I was going to have to struggle to make my way within the community of kindergarten.

To put it more plainly, I was going to have to fight. And in a certain very real sense, I've been fighting ever since, through childhood, adulthood, and finally and triumphantly, many years later, in the courtroom as well.

CHAPTER

4

How to Find a Lawyer;
Mediation Vs. Court; From the
Lawyers Point of View:
Legal Impressions of a Client
Named Vira Goldman

CHAPTER 4

I T WAS SEVEN MONTHS AFTER ROBERT PACKED HIS bags and left our house that I had my first meeting with Norman Sheresky and Allan Mayefsky, the lawyers who would become my divorce lawyers. I was at the time still searching for a lawyer to handle my case, and I remember this initial meeting clearly. We sat down at a table in their offices and began conversationally hashing out the pros and cons of my situation. Norman, as senior partner of Sheresky Aronson & Mayefsky, gave me his thoughts on going into litigation (as opposed to negotiating a settlement). At a certain point, very casually, Norman threw out a number, a percentage of what I might expect from a judgement.

This was before the "discovery," as it's called, during which time the finances of the couple are vetted. No one but myself actually knew the numbers at that time. But Norman threw out an approximate number based on speculation and the legal precedents governing what women have typically gotten in such cases. Norman has a comfortable, put-you-at-ease manner, which conceals what is in fact a lightning fast legal mind. After mentioning this figure, he leaned back in his chair confidently.

I leaned forward and said, "Norman, don't you ever tell a lady what her settlement will be. She's gonna tell YOU."

Well, with that, Norman, still leaning back on his chair, started to laugh. I laughed, too, we said our good-byes, and I then left for Europe.

While I was abroad, I found myself thinking about them and deciding that despite the disagreement in their conference room, there was enough intelligence and power between the two of them so that we might still make a good match. Plus, I knew Norman's background well and had met him before socially and liked him, which was an added inducement. Sheresky Aronson & Mayefsky were familiar to me as among the nation's leading family law practitioners. Allan I didn't know at all, and in the conference room he was very quiet. Of course, I couldn't really know if they were for me until I actually sat down with them and began to work, but when I came back, my mind was made up, and I had decided to give it a try.

One of my incentives in getting the best lawyers that I could find was that I had seen several of my women friends get divorced, and I had been appalled by how they had gone about it. One friend in particular had supported her husband for many years. He had an alcohol problem, and she was a hardworking woman who kept the home together, protected the family, and hid his drinking problem from the world as best she could. He came from a well-off family, and she had nothing, and when they finally split, she had nothing to fall back on. But *he* did. He knew that during the divorce he'd be getting his father's house and would eventually inherit money from his parents. I felt that she should have the marital home, free and clear, as a minimum. Just keep the house, no matter what, I kept advising her. But as so many women are at a moment like this, she was demoralized and not particularly focused, and so she hemmed and hawed and said, "Well my lawyer thought..." I responded: "Nevermind what your lawyer thought. You've gotta be the activator and tell him what you want. And furthermore tell him from the outset: if you can't do it, then I don't want you as my lawyer." This is merely commonsense, I told her. It's not even business sense, it's plain old-fashioned common sense that I've always had and that I gave to my husband too. Every one of us has a basic dose of it, and when you develop that common sense, it eventually becomes a guiding logic that will keep you out of the worst that life throws at you.

Pick and Choose: the Process of Selecting Your Lawyer

My own philosophy, as I repeat throughout this book, is that a good divorce is a quick divorce. That is, once officially begun, the machinery of divorce should work as efficiently as possible toward its end: just distribution of property and assets, a fair and mutual agreement about the children, and the end of the marriage. Divorces that drag on seem eventually to take on the qualities of a lingering illness: they gradually wear you down to no good end.

Many people have hesitations about going to get a lawyer in the first place. They fight getting one because they believe it signals, once and for all, that they are about to get divorced, and part of them still doesn't want to admit this fact.

Unfortunately, the law isn't interested in your hesitation. When contemplating a divorce, a cardinal rule under the circumstances is: don't wait until it's too late to find a lawyer. Don't wait, that is, until you're so emotionally battered and the process itself is so far along that you can no longer think straight. Everything to do with finding a lawyer should be as methodical and efficient as possible. Also, if you go to a lawyer early, you can obtain the pre-separation advice that can be so useful for you.

A divorce procedure is not pretty, and comes down to this basic fact: the court has the power to take everything away from you, house, money, children—EVERYTHING. The job of the attorney your spouse has hired is to find compelling reasons to make the court do just that.

The job of your lawyer is to defend you. Are you getting the picture? Divorce is adversarial. No matter how elegantly phrased the arguments used, it is a fight—especially if it goes to court. You must protect yourself by planning well ahead.

Women sometimes think: well, I'm a successful person; I have a job; I don't drink or smoke or carouse—OF COURSE I'll get child custody. Not necessarily true! There are two sides to every argument, and no matter who you are or how you lead your life, you must remember that you have no control over the judge who is assigned your case, and it's entirely possible that this judge will have a value system different from yours and sees things in a way that shocks and disappoints you. A good divorce lawyer, who undertakes your case with intelligence and vigor, is your only real defense.

How do you go about finding this good lawyer?

There are several different ways. Some people simply canvas their friends or co-workers. Others ask their therapists, because therapists, who often deal with divorce, tend to know divorce lawyers. If you already have a lawyer you know and like who works in a related field, he will probably give you a dependable name. You can even, as some enterprising women have done, search for a lawyer among the records of the court where your divorce case will be litigated. These records are available to the public, and any interested parties can actually go and study the details. You can also simply go watch local divorce trials, observe litigating lawyers in action, and approach one you like.

Yet another possibility is to contact a referral service sponsored by the local bar association. Most American states have them. Remember that most lawyers listed with referral services are only there because they paid a fee to be placed on the list. After you get their names, you still have to interview them closely.

As to those lawyers who advertise on television or magazines: these lawyers have what are known as "volume" practices. Vast numbers of people come to them, based on these ads, and they, the lawyers, choose which of the clients will be the easiest and most lucrative cases. Excuse me, but that is all-over backward. *You* are hiring *them*, not the other way around. These kind of assembly line lawyers are best avoided in favor of those lawyers who will give you a more personalized, detail-oriented kind of service.

After you have drawn up a list of likely candidates, you can then begin the interviewing process. Don't forget that when you go into the interview for a lawyer, *you* are conducting the interview, not the other way around. The lawyer is a vendor of a service. In this, he is like a plumber or a locksmith, with an important difference: you will be working with him closely, revealing intimate details of your life, and will be most likely spending large amounts of time in his or her presence. Make your choice accordingly. Are you comfortable with the lawyer? Does he condescend to you? Or does he give you the impression of friendly, intelligent participation in your case? Is he giving you a hard-sell about his qualities, "pitching" you on his indispensability, or does he give you a balanced sense of himself?

Here are some good basic background questions to ask prospective lawyers.

- ✦ How much of your practice is in domestic relations law, and how long have you been doing it?
- ✦ Aside from matrimonial cases, what other kinds of law do you practice?
- ✦ What were two of your cases that were important to you, and why?

You should also ask the following basic financial questions:

- ✦ How much do you charge?
- ✦ Do you request an advance retainer?
- ✦ How much do you estimate my case will cost?
- ✦ How long do you estimate it will take to bring to completion?
- ✦ Are your fees negotiable?

Another useful line of inquiry is to ask the lawyer if he or she has published any books or magazine articles dealing with the field of domestic relations. This will give you a quick sense of the lawyer's commitment, and if you read the articles, they will serve as a good outside reference for the lawyer's state of mind.

Be organized. Take notes of your impressions of the lawyers. Keep a journal. Phone the various candidates first, and explain, as clearly as possible, what it is you're seeking and why. If, after a phone conversation, you are still interested in meeting the lawyer face to face, then you've saved yourself a wasted appointment.

Remember: most lawyers will charge you for that initial meeting. The fact that you're paying to interview the lawyer should be all the incentive you need to be as organized as possible, and make every minute of that face to face meeting pay dividends for you. Don't allow the lawyer to digress overly, and end the interview when you think you've gathered as much information as you need. You're the boss. The lawyer, I repeat (and repeat, and repeat) works for you. Would you hire an employee without properly checking out his references? You should do the same with a lawyer.

When I went to get a lawyer, I already knew that the kind of lawyer I had, along with his/her preparation and experience, would be crucial in the eventual outcome of my case. A good lawyer has a creative mind, and a fanatically detailed knowledge of legal precedent; he is able to apply his vast knowledge to the issues at hand, and do so quickly. A divorce trial, after all, is rarely open and shut. Rather it is often a drawn-out saga of interpretation. And the lawyer's role is to cajole, beguile, insist, and parade hard-headed facts in such a way that the judge, or jury, is swayed.

When it comes to lawyers, and specifically divorce lawyers, the phrase to keep in mind is, "with all due speed." You want a lawyer with a creative mind and a deep understanding of the law, who is willing to work efficiently on your behalf, but not so fast that the process becomes a blur, and you lose sight of the details. But not so slow that he drags things out that could easily have been dealt with more quickly.

A good lawyer, like my lawyers Norman and Allan, must have a wide background in the law, a creative mind, and a deep intellect. He (or she) must be able both to argue, know all the possible legal precedents, and be convincing when speaking.

The "climate" you establish in your interview with the lawyer is a key indicator of the eventual successful outcome of the case. You must, from the start, establish an atmosphere of mutual respect and credibility—because it is that which produces team spirit. If you read through this book, you'll know how hard I worked with my two lawyers to establish that spirit of mutual respect. Once I had done so, and things were clear between us, we could all pull together towards our common goal.

In my case, I first had recourse to a trust and estates lawyer, a man who was recommended to me as a tremendous negotiator. And, since I, like so many other people who institute divorce proceedings, was hoping to negotiate a settlement, he seemed like the right man for the job. Everything was out front, the numbers were all a matter of public record, and my hope was that we could simply break everything down the middle and get on with our lives.

The trust and estates lawyer came at the very beginning of the eight-month "breathing space" I had allowed Robert, during which time he might live on his own without me and let the fact of a divorce sink in. From that moment on, during that entire eight- month period, this lawyer was trying to negotiate a settlement. I wanted things to move slowly during this period, so that Robert could digest the fact that there was going to be a divorce. So, for almost eight months time, the divorce case proceeded very slowly. But the bottom line soon became clear: we could not agree, and as such, we would have to litigate.

Mediation Vs Court

Now, I know I'm unusual in this, but I'm built that way, and there's no use denying it: I wanted to go to court. I'm a scrapper, and I love a good dust-up, and as I've said already, the strategy, the drama, and the steady march toward victory in my particular trial exhilarated me. Not everybody is built that way, of course, and in fact only a small percentage of divorce cases actually make it to trial. Most are settled out of court, sometimes on the courthouse steps on the day of the trial! Many others are resolved in the offices of a mediator.

Mediation, also known as "alternative dispute resolution" or "assisted negotiation," involves sitting down with your spouse in a neutral meeting room and hashing out your conflicting claims under the trained supervision of a mediator. It's a process of communication and compromise among warring parties, and it's gradually changing the rough-and-tumble nature of traditional-style divorce. Mediation, because it's about talking things out, often makes for a more kinder, gentler divorce than the old-fashioned courtroom combat. And because it's an analytic process, with the two divorcing partners having a direct hand in the resolution of their marriage, it tends to avoid the kind of emotional bloodshed that is bad for the children caught in the middle.

Mediators most often are appointed by the court, usually with agreement by the lawyers for both sides. Professional private mediators, many of whom are lawyers, eliminate the need for a jury trial about ninety percent of the time. Although most people don't learn about mediation options until after a divorce decree has been filed, a savvy few seek out Dispute Resolution Services first. When they reach agreement on the terms of the divorce, they take it to an attorney who drafts the decree and files it at great cost savings.

Total confidentiality and neutrality are the cornerstones of the mediation process. And when mediation fails, people still have the courts available.

If you go the route of mediation, an important thing to remember is that the mediator is not YOUR advocate. He or she is a professional engaged by the couple of which you are one half. If you feel, within the mediation, for whatever reason, that you are not able to represent yourself fully, then don't hesitate to ask for representation. Also, a mediation is not a forum in which to vent your anger. Mediation instead is a process based on compromise, and if the two of you have hardened your positions, and are looking for a battle royale, then the courtroom is where you'll most certainly end up

By the way, there is a downside to mediation too: a vengeful spouse bent on prolonging the agony of a divorce can easily manipulate the mediation system, drawing out the process and tormenting his or her partner at the same time. In a situation like this, a smart lawyer could bring the grinding agony to a quick halt.

Whether it be mediation or the kind of courtroom drama which was my experience, you are always best served if you think of your divorce as an active process in which you must take a direct hand. Instead of passively going through the motions, try adopting the dynamic attitude of an entrepreneur. After all, when business people start a new company, they go to the lawyers only AFTER they have done their own investigating and assessed all the risks and rewards of the investment. In the same way, you should prepare the ground before you go to the lawyers or mediators. Don't expect the legal system to take care of you because it is not designed to do that. The only person who can take care of you in a divorce is you yourself: so be methodical, start early, and think positive!

All this above advice is the fruit of hard-earned experience. And it was experience gained working principally with Norman and Allan—though not only them. I've had recourse to many lawyers in my years in business, and I've learned, for example, that it's always best to arrive in a lawyer's office with a lot of things written down. Their legal training inclines them to take anything written very seriously, more so than verbal conversation. Therefore, whenever you can, give it to them in writing. If you want to keep records of your individual phone calls to them, so much the better.

Then, self-presentation. Too many times women contemplating a divorce arrive at the lawyer's office and display the worst of themselves. Men may too, but I'm writing this book for women, and it's women's cases I know best. Too often they arrive in the lawyer's office distraught and confused, and really, that's the most damaging state a woman can be in. That's why I want you, the reader, to take careful note here: you must realize that not only is the lawyer auditioning for you, but you for the lawyer. You must be prepared, level-headed, and rational. You must enter that office with a plan, an overall goal, and, hopefully, an at least vague sense of the strategy that got you there.

With Norman and Allan, despite my preparation and what I thought to have been an air-clearing initial conversation, things weren't exactly hunky-dory at first. As smart and able as they were, they were simply unused to a woman pulling her weight at this level. I felt my vital input was disregarded. I felt I was being left out of crucial decisions that were my right to help make. Weeks would go by, and I wouldn't hear anything from them. It wasn't a specific incident so much as it was a general climate of keeping me out of the loop.

What did I do? What I always do: I fought. I was determined to get my legal due. When I first raised objections to Allan, he said, "If you raise your voice to me, then who can I raise my voice to?"

"Certainly not your wife," I said. "How about Norman?" We both laughed, and that put everything back at ease.

It took awhile, but my insistence on being included in the strategy sessions led them slowly to accept me as a full partner in our case. Then, still early on in our preparations, we came to the crucial moment: they asked me, what percent would you settle for? I said, exactly what I deserve, fifty percent. I still remember the look of shocked disbelief that flashed across their faces before they composed themselves. I knew why: because I was going up against a long-standing legal precedent that discourages equal distribution of a couple's wealth in high-profile divorce cases (high profile means anything more than about fifteen million dollars). In their eyes, I was asking for something that was almost impossible, even if I'm a brunette with brown eyes and a not bad body (great legs).

Allan and I did a kind of call and response, as I remember. He was the one who was actually "building" the case, i.e. assembling the lines of argument, and he would say, "Vira, would you take forty percent if Robert offered it as a settlement?" Absolutely not, I'd answer cheerfully. "forty-five percent?" he'd ask hopefully. "No way," I'd say. One night late, walking me to the elevator, he gave the question again, and asked me, somewhat pleadingly: "Vira, would you accept forty-seven percent?" "Now Allan," I said sweetly, "I know you're having a hard time with this, so I want to make it as easy as I can for you. This is what I want you to do. Each night, when you get into bed and put your head on your soft down pillow, I want you to repeat, Vira is getting fifty percent, Vira is getting fifty percent, Vira is getting fifty percent. Believe me, you'll never need to ask this question again." I got into the elevator and I said "good night and sweet dreams."

Fifty percent became the fixed amount toward which we would push from then on.

From the Lawyer's Point of View: Legal Impressions of a Client

Vira first entered our offices as an extremely pleasant, highly focused woman who seemed to know exactly what she wanted. What she wanted was a divorce; she was not interested in a reconciliation. She said the point had been reached between her and her husband in which they were so far away from one another that it was time to go their separate ways. She mentioned that she was displeased that after thirty-three years of being a caretaker and putting him first and creating a family environment, he had relegated her financially to the status of upstairs maid. She had been, she explained, his equal partner, and wanted to be vindicated in this belief.

Working with her on the case was a combination of exhilaration and exasperation. Vira is a capable woman who was highly focused and never asked extraneous questions. On the other hand, for a significant period of time during the preparation of the case, she seemed to think that she could also be a capable and competent lawyer. She wanted to control the process, for example, as regards the granting or withholding of adjournments, scheduling, etc. She wanted copies of everything including the trivial. But she also knew her stuff. She was able to document verbally and otherwise her countless contributions to the marriage and to recall the minutia which goes into building a successful case. She became angry on a number of occasions when she didn't like what we proposed or didn't like the way we proposed it. She constantly bristled at the notion that it might be smarter to talk about settlement than go through the rigors of a trial. On the other hand, she was cooperative and after sufficient debates usually went along with pretrial and trial strategy.

One of the things that will remain with us was how clear she was in her objectives. Many clients who come to our offices are goal-driven. But few seem to have a comprehensive plan, to arrive determined not to surrender control of their lives to their lawyers. In Vira's case, she did this by organizing and presenting her life to her lawyers in her History of My Marriage, a biographical sketch which we then helped edit, organize and present in legalese so as to both explain the life and finances of a family and place a clear emphasis and focus on Vira's contributions to the final results. As

*in all cases, the seemingly trivial can make an enormous differ-
ence, and several of these biographical details proved key in the
trial. For example, the fact that Vira gave Bob Goldman haircuts
every few weeks probably was as important in making her case as
the six houses she built and designed. Every case has several of such
incredibly important little facts that can be burned in the memo-
ry of a court, but they have to be dug out. In Vira's case, she was
full of such nuggets. An important point to remember here is that
Vira, to an unusual degree, sought our advice, used our advice, but
was not beguiled by it. She retained a sharp, independent point of
view, and vetted everything we proposed through her own common
sense. This relationship works both ways, of course: lawyers, too,
must be careful to use the facts their clients give them, and not be
beguiled by the client's logic or pet theories. The point is that the
facts must ring true to not only the client, but to the court also.*

*By the end of the case, I think Vira will agree, we had achieved
an unusually sharp team focus and harmony of ideas. The process
worked pretty darn well, and the facts, as facts always do, speak for
themselves.*

Norman and Allan

CHAPTER

5

Meeting and Marrying Robert;
Discovering the World of Business Together;
The Nature of our Partnership

CHAPTER 5

FIFTY PERCENT. HALF. A FULLY EQUAL SHARE. TO achieve such a thing a woman would have to prove that she had had as important a contribution as a man to the making of the worth and value of a family. She would have to convince the trial judge that the role formally known as "woman's work" was as important as the man's role of being out in the world. To do so she would have to explain something of the background of the couple of which she was a fully equal partner, a couple, which like just about every couple, met, courted, and fell in love.

As I've said, I didn't pass all that much time in childhood involved in romantic dreams of marriage. To me, marriage as a girl meant partnership, in emulation of my parent's marriage, with its organized rhythms, its feeling of teamwork, and its deep, silent, and abiding love.

By the time I decided to get married, I was well "out" of

Rochester, the city of my birth. I had in fact been teaching kindergarten for several years, carrying a full-time job and living in Manhattan. My life was outwardly fulfilled, but I felt an inner voice telling me in clear terms that it was time: time to settle down with a man and start a family. And—at the ripe old age of 27—I felt ready to begin the adventure.

Having decided I was ready, I looked around and chose the best of the bunch. The best of the bunch was a shy, handsome, very gentlemanly man named Robert Goldman who seemed to have the inside track on making me laugh. An intelligent and level-headed soul, he was working for his father in a factoring business, and seemed the ideal match for me. He was well educated, could talk about everything, was informed and up to date. He was alert to trends and provided a comfortable, secure feeling. He was also a fantastic listener who seemed to have the ability to enter into me and draw out my inner self. Used as I was to men on dates bragging about themselves, I was impressed by this courtly, old-fashioned man with impeccable manners. From the start, he was as punctual and dependable as a clock. I never had to wonder where he was, or why. His word was law. If he said so, he delivered.

Robert didn't want a wedding, so, after talking it over, we decided to elope. It meant disappointing my parents, who weren't there at the "ceremony," which was, as I recall, held on December 31, 1964. I had a little Volkswagen, and I went around and picked him up at his office in Manhattan, and then we went to the jewelry district to select our rings. Mine was a gold band that cost fourteen bucks. We jumped back into the VW and drove to Greenwich, Connecticut, where we were married before a man named Judge Frost, in his own house. I wore a cream-colored lace suit, black suede boots, and a beautiful antique green-embroidered handbag that Robert had given me on one of our dates. And that was my wedding outfit. Robert wore a pinstriped dark business suit. When we asked the Judge where to spend the weekend on our "honeymoon," he suggested the town of Silvermine, and as we left, gave us the following parting blessing: "You know," he said helpfully, "most of these kind of weddings don't last." Ignoring this unhappy prediction, we drove to Silvermine, checked into the tavern, went to dinner, and then to see a James Bond movie, "To Live and Let Die." So much for veils and bridesmaids. The adventure of my marriage had begun.

It didn't take us long to settle down. We moved into my tiny apartment on East 83rd Street and quickly found matching rhythms. Our backgrounds as Ashkenazi Jew and Ukrainian were very similar in certain ways, and in fact, with my childhood among Jewish friends and neighbors, I knew more about some of his traditions than he did!

I loved the stable rhythms and certainties of marriage. The days ran like clockwork. Each morning I'd leave to teach school in Irvington, a lovely old town a half-hour up the Hudson, and Robert would head off downtown to work. Dinnertime, we'd gather in the apartment to hash over the day's events. We both had plenty of homework to deal with in the evenings, and between that, socializing, the theatre, and the first blush of marriage, all ran smoothly.

As to religious observance, we got around our differences in the best and most-time tested way: compromise. We each went to each other's religious services on respective holy holidays and were satisfied with that. I'm not threatened by being in a foreign religious environment, and I in fact loved the services, the prayers, the atmosphere, and the philosophy espoused in the synagogue. All of the religions of the world, after all, are built on the same foundation.

From the very beginning of our marriage, it was obvious that Robert would rely on me on a daily basis, and not merely for the comforts and organization of a home—though of course for that too. No, he would rely on me for advice, input, and counsel in the love of his life: his business. I was raised by a father who instructed me at a very early age in the methodical approach to problem solving and by a mother who had a keen instinct for financial dealings. I had both those qualities within myself, allied to practical know-how and a deep competitive streak. It would have been foolish of Robert to ignore the resource he had at hand—a resource who happened to be married to him besides. Early on, before we had our child, before I discovered my talents as a designer and restorer of houses and a collector of eighteenth-century antiques and art, before we really had any money at all, he brought me into the world of his business, and we discovered in our discussions and mutual support a new kind of marital creativity.

One of the first things Robert did when he met me was give me his business card with the words "vice president" written on it. Needless to say, I was plenty impressed at the time. Later, of course, I would learn that there were only ten people in the entire company, but at the time it seemed a very refined and important a position to hold.

The reality, at least at the time of our marriage, was that Robert, with all his advanced degrees and acumen, had parked the car of his ambition in a pretty cramped spot. He had been an academic whiz in college, Phi Betta Kappa in his junior year at Harvard, and then onto Yale Law. But he soon grew turned off by the argumentative combat of law practice and began casting about for an alternative. His father, knowing of his dissatisfaction, asked him to come aboard the family business, and Robert did. And in so doing, he found his life-long work.

At the time Robert came into the company, Congress Factors, as it was called, consisted of a sleepy fledgling operation which did "factoring", i.e. making short-term loans to businesses who require money in the time gap between shipping goods and receiving payment. It is a business that requires a keen nose for calculation and an intuitive sense of market trends.

This was fine in and of itself, and it was a business with distinct growth possibilities. But the easy-going gentlemen who ran it (Robert's father and two other men) were trained in a different area of business and relied completely on one man to run the company—an arrangement that put them in a vulnerable position. This man, as it turns out, was an indifferent businessman, and was finally removed, but the company was still in bad straits when Robert took over.

From the first, there was entirely open communication between us about the business. This was not casual chat, but serious, searching conversation. Not that we didn't have fun, and laugh our heads off sometimes, but there was a sense that we were in this together, and we must put our heads together and make the corporation go.

I'm aware that this kind of marital partnership is not exactly common, and was even less so in my generation, when men went to work and women stayed home and kept house. But be that as it may, Robert shared everything with me, as well he should have. That early period in the business was very shaky, and there was a feeling that a single misstep could have sent the company crashing to the ground.

My advice to him was that he take the bull by the horns, clean house and restructure the company. This was not advanced calculus, this was simple common sense. The place was littered with the deadwood of mistaken hires and people inappropriate to their positions. But it wasn't only specific decisions I advised him on. I tried in general to convince him to take a guiding, proactive role in the business, rather than simply sit back and let himself be led. Having grown up a self-motivating child, I worked to instill that same attitude in my husband. My nature is to mother—but with some fire in the mother's milk! There's nothing wrong with a little aggression, especially in the world of business, where so many people are only after what they can get out of you.

To his credit, Robert was confident enough to allow me to have my say. He wasn't threatened by me. After all, he saw the neatness and organization of our home, and used to stand back and marvel at my speed as a housekeeper. And in our discussions, I would never let Robert think he wasn't anything but the top dog. The core of a good marriage, after all, is that it builds up both principals, rather than tears them down. In our marriage, I made it clear to Robert that he was the star. In this, I was only being truthful. Robert had an uncanny knack for calculating numbers at lightning speed and intuiting the behavior of companies in the volatile world of high finance. At the same time he was patient, stable and very honest, and a true gentlemen—these were the qualities by which he was known by everyone who ever dealt with him. His motto, appropriately enough, was "slow and steady."

In our discussions I didn't argue. Arguing with him was not my style. There are many ways a wife and husband communicate, some obvious, some implicit, and my preferred style was to plant the seeds and let him discover the fruit. And a hundred times over the years, when he was having troubles with his business, we'd sit down together and patiently work through the issues involved.

In another life I would have done the exact same thing with my husband the plumber, my husband the pizza maker, or my husband the car mechanic. But my husband in THIS life happened to be a businessman, and so my contributions tended to revolve around the world of Congress Financial Corporation.

A lot of our conversations took place when we were driving. In fact, it became kind of a joke between us and got to the point that when we were about to have a business chat, we'd say, "OK, let's talk business, let's get into the car." It was on one of those drives that Robert first broached to me what I've since come privately to refer to as The Philadelphia Story. You see, in the early years of the company Robert was searching for a senior partner to invest in Congress, and the best prospect at the time was the Philadelphia National Bank. This bank eventually came up with a deal that seemed fine on paper save for one thing: they wanted the main office relocated away from Manhattan and to—where else—Philadelphia. At this time Congress Factors worked exclusively with 7th Avenue clients, i.e. people in the retail garment business, so it seemed on the surface a little strange to be moving the main office a hundred miles away from the client base. I still remember the day Robert came home and announced that he was being wooed by the Philly National Bank and that we might end up moving to Philadelphia. We had just recently purchased our first house in Irvington in Hudson, New York. The house itself was situated in a beautiful little green dell not far from the Hudson River, and I'd carefully supervised a labor-intensive renovation. Robert, I said, there are two things that do not under any circumstances belong in Philadelphia. The first is Congress, the other is ME. I added: I just left a very provincial town, and I can't see myself going back to another provincial town. Besides, it makes no sense on a business level.

The truth is, I was shocked that Robert was even entertaining such a thought. I mean, if little old me sitting in her house could understand that this made no sense professionally, why couldn't he? But Robert was very excited by the offer from a bank this large, and prevailed on me to spend an experimental weekend in Philadelphia. So we drove down, took a hotel, and decided to check out the extent of the social and cultural life. We came in on a Friday, as I recall, and went to a nightclub of sorts, which had horrible amateur singers belting out show tunes. After sitting through that, grimacing, we went out to a tasteless dinner. The next morning, we woke up, looked at each other, and said, How about a quick return trip to NYC?

While we were driving back, I said, Robert, if you really think this a great business decision, then we'll have to somehow get a *pied a terre* in New York, because I can't cut my connections to that city. The truth is, I felt much more strongly than my comment might have indicated. I didn't want to move to Philadelphia in the least. But would I tell him that? No, that's not my way. I didn't get hysterical or forbid him. I don't give ultimatums and never will. My way from the beginning has always been to negotiate, to look at all the options, do some give and take, and then to let things lie fallow, with the hope that the person will eventually see the light.

This was my style, my personal method. I wanted to empower Robert to come to his own decisions. I wanted him to be in the limelight. I was the caregiver. This was fine with me. I had total self-confidence, and didn't need to throw myself showily out in the world. We had evolved a give-and-take relationship, Robert and I, a relationship in which I was doing my job at one end, and he at the other. I wanted Robert to be a success. Success, after all, was very important to me. And I was certain I was going to be successful in life whether alone or with someone else.

After much soul-searching, Robert decided to turn down the offer from the Philly National Bank. I was very happy about that one, let me tell you! And so the search went on for a senior partner. And, in the way of such things, six months later the same Philadelphia bank came back to him with a different deal, whose terms were better across the board. In addition, there was the added pleasure that the main office would now stay in New York, and only a branch annex would open in Philly. The deal was made, and Philadelphia National Bank became the senior partner of Congress Factors. I was asked to decorate the offices and happily obliged. It was the beginning of my work decorating the office space of Congress Financial Corporation as it grew over the next thirty years.

The reason I tell this story at a certain length is because of the following fact: not long after they opened the branch office in Philadelphia, it closed. When Robert came home one evening and told me the news, I said, My god, that could have been the entire company! Nodding somewhat sorrowfully, he agreed, and then added, "the truth is, Vira, if you hadn't been there urging me not to, I probably would have gone ahead with that earlier deal, and God knows where we would be now!"

Where we would have been was in financial straits, most likely. Instead, Congress Factors began slowly and steadily to gain speed. Not that we weren't apprehensive in those early years. We were, and for good reason: because we were starting at rock bottom. A lot was hanging in the balance, day to day, week to week. In such situations, you tend to focus hard on concrete issues, on little details. What you don't do is slap yourself on the back and get full of self-congratulatory euphoria over the fact you have a growing business. You don't want to dwell on how great things are going, because to do so, as Robert explained to me, is to give yourself a *canahora* (Yiddish for bad luck).

Robert's philosophy was if something good is coming toward you, you don't ever look it straight in the eye. This was perfectly in line with the self-effacing side of the rest of his character. Robert was a fiercely focused businessman, but he never tooted his horn, ever. In fact, he couldn't even bring himself to set financial goals because he was afraid it would jinx them. Of course the company was striving to do better, but he simply refused to set projections. I, on the other hand, had no such superstitions. OK, I would say firmly, now we're making a profit of X dollars a month, let's try for Y by this time

70

next year. A year later, looking somewhat abashed, he would quietly tell me that I had reason to be happy: Y, in fact, had been reached.

It wasn't easy in those early years. As in all businesses, there were problems of bad debts, clients going broke and Congress getting stuck for a lot of money. But fortunately, the solvent clients outweighed the bankrupt ones, and the company continued to grow. Eventually to the factoring side of things was added commercial finance, and in the early '80s the company really took wing, with offices opening so rapidly around the country I could barely keep tabs on them all.

Part of the reason for the rise of the company was the presence of a superb team of partners, men of vision and insight who, along with Robert, grew right along with the company and were key to its success. Through it all, Robert's smooth, imperturbable character remained unaffected. Despite the invariable ups and downs, his routine was fixed early on and stayed that way. After dinner, during which we discussed the events of the day, he would sit on his favorite spot—the sofa in the dressing room, furnished in American eighteenth century—and there read his "homework". He would go to bed very early, about 9:30 or ten, and I would stay up another couple of hours.

Robert was a highly organized man. So organized in fact, that he would be one of those individuals who if, god forbid, he'd ever lost his sight, would have an entirely smooth transition. He would know exactly where everything was because he did the exact same thing every day.

When it came to business, he organized his professional life with the same precision and care. He gave out the message that he expected things done promptly and efficiently. And yet in the office he was a gentleman, he was fair, he listened, he never kept the door of his office closed, but kept it open to every employee. Everybody loved working for Robert, and his staff had nothing but good things to say about him.

Despite his smooth outer surface, however, Robert was a born worrier. He could never shake this inclination to be pre-occupied. It was as much a part of him as the color of his hair. He worried all the time, and he never slept peacefully through the night, for that reason.

That said, he never worried about me. He had a ton of confidence in me, and for the best of reasons: because I gave it to him. I was there. I was a rock. You don't worry about the rock. It may wear a bit around the edges, but the structure will still be there.

My own goal was to provide as secure, warm and nourishing a home as possible and to do my best to make my husband successful in his work and life. Are these outmoded aspirations? I don't think so! Everybody, no matter who they are, needs a warm nest, a secure environment, a place to return to at the end of the day, in which they can relax, open their heart, and recharge their energies. I did my very best to make sure that Robert Goldman left the house each morning with a contented glow and was operating at 100 percent. I was his catalyst, his energizer, his wife and lover, and I was also his confidante, his advisor, his troubleshooter, and his fiercest defender.

During the early period of the company, I recall him saying to me, "I never realized how ambitious you are." And he was right. I would settle for nothing less then complete success. He needed the push. And it worked.

For many years, Robert and I were happy together. We had a clear sense of purpose and a goal: two things which are as important in a marriage as they are in anything else in life. We functioned well in the corporate environments in which we sometimes had to socialize (even if Robert was not especially outgoing, and was happier noodling around the house than going out on the town), and enjoyed each other's company.

Then, slowly, the enthusiasm began to leak away. I've already sketched out how as he began to contract, I began to expand. I was running a very satisfying and well-developed business in historic preservation. I was outwardly fulfilled in my work and my daughter was growing into a wonderful person. But even as my life swept forward, I couldn't help but feel that Robert was remaining frozen in place. People this age are slowing down, Robert kept saying, but you are speeding up. I can't keep up with you, he added. And that was what was happening. I was looking to the future and beginning to flower. Robert was treading water, and the water seemed to be rising.

CHAPTER

6

The History of Divorce

CHAPTER 6

I KNEW THAT IN ASKING FOR FULLY FIFTY PERCENT, I was not only shocking my lawyers and going up against a long-standing precedent. What I didn't know, until I began looking into it, was just *how* long-standing a precedent it was.

The history of divorce can be stated simply: things started out very badly for women, and they've been getting better very slowly ever since. How badly were they at the beginning? In Ancient Greece, women couldn't be *seen* in public. For another 1,500 years, women could be sold like a bag of potatoes or a sack of grain. It's important to remember that during much of that time, the Church fathers held sway. Actually, the Catholic Church has been remarkably consistent in its view of women, and that view has been negative. Not only did the church forbid divorce for centuries, but it contributed to the climate in which women were invisible, or worse, guilty of a terrible crime in simply being female. It wasn't an accident that Eve was blamed for man's downfall from the Garden of Eden. In the fourth century, one of the learned Church fathers, St. Jerome, put it this way: "Woman is the gate of the devil, the path of wickedness, the sting of the serpent, in a word a perilous object." Nine centuries later, things hadn't improved all that much. Thomas Aquinas, a church father of the thirteenth century, wrote: "woman was created to be man's helpmeet, but her unique role is in conception . . . since for other purposes men would be better assisted by other men."

For many centuries, women had no legal status at all. The man was her "lord and master," she did his bidding upon pain of punishment, and not even her death was recorded. Generation after generation, women went to their graves unaware that there was slow progress being made, and that their struggles were very gradually bearing fruit.

We ourselves forget, of course. We forget we stand on the shoulders of all those silent, unknown women who came before us, women who struggled in their own lives for their basic human rights and were denied them. We forget how recent is our legal status as equals to men. We take for granted the immense amount of privilege we have, compared to these ancestors.

In the words of another friend of women, Sir William Blackstone, the famed eighteenth-century British legal eagle, "Husband and wife are one, and that one is the husband."

Britain, that cradle of Western Civilization, does not have a particularly pretty history as regards the treatment of wives. In eleventh-century Britain, men were more or less free to step out on their wives, but if a British rose were to do the same thing to her husband her nose and ears would be cut off by the indignant magistrate! As recently as the eighteenth-century in Britain, a man could sell his wife on the open market. All the doting hubby had to do was "put a halter about her neck and thereby lead her to the next market place, and there put her up to auction to be sold to the best bidder."

American divorce law is an inheritance from England, considerably modernized for its debut in the New World. The main difference? American divorce developed without the long, disapproving shadow of the Church hanging over it. The Pilgrims who landed on Plymouth Rock had practical, relatively modern ideas about how to uncouple, and decided that for the first time in history, divorce would be a civil, not a church matter, and that it would be done quickly as well.

Another difference was that in democratic America, anybody could get divorced, rich or poor. For a long time in Europe, only the very wealthy, those from "great families," could pull strings, pay off the right people, and get divorced. In the US, by contrast, the option was available to most everybody.

And the option was used. Divorce in America was a boom industry in the early days, peaking around the time of the Civil War. All the traditional disruptions of war caused a sharp spike in divorces, and foreigners arriving in America were amazed at the spectacle of how easy and quick it was to undo what "god hath put together." This was still, statistically, nothing compared to what would come in the future.

In 1931, Reno Nevada, the capital of the quickie divorce, hung out its shingle. But in the 1930s and '40s, divorce in America was still regarded as something deeply negative. In the words of a sociology textbook of that time, "Divorce is the public acknowledgement of failure."

By the late 1950s, the enormous wave of prosperity that had begun after the war started to change American society. Americans began to turn away from their traditional obligations to family and community and became more individualistic, more interested in throwing off tradition and expressing themselves. In the 1960s, divorce in America became a boom industry.

This was for many social reasons, but there was also a very concrete one. The advent of no-fault laws had streamlined the process, and taken a lot of the nastiness away. Up until then, divorce laws always contained a long, pointing index finger that blamed one or the other of the partners for the marital meltdown. Sometimes, as in my home state of New York, the earlier divorce laws also required that one spouse demonstrate that the other had engaged in adultery or any of a variety of divorceable crimes. This produced an avalanche of often hilarious scenes. Did the judge want mental cruelty? Alright, your lawyer would whisper to you, just tell the court your husband called you names. Did the judge want physical cruelty? OK, then your lawyer would call a recess, and you'd come back in a few minutes, carefully coached, and say your husband had just slapped you. In addition to this, to prove adultery, thousands of couples had to concoct "posed" scenes in hotel rooms, with flash photographers hired for the occasions.

It shows you just how ridiculous an outmoded law can be—that it causes people to go to these lengths, to lie and invent wholesale fabrications to get something which both of them—wife and husband—want: the end of their marriage.

The '60s divorce boom, by the way, happened in every country of the industrialized West, but was most pronounced in (you guessed it) England, which experienced an astonishing *doubling* of divorces between 1960 and 1970. It was almost as if the historical ghost of British women, having been denied its voice for a thousand years, had decided to wreak its revenge in court.

At the same time as the number of divorces shot through the roof, the stigma attached to the act itself, carefully nurtured over centuries of Catholic guilt and shame, fell away like an old flaking coat of paint. At the beginning of the second millenium, one out of two Americans now call it quits and end their marriage.

The new climate around divorce reflects a larger social change, which could be called The Recognition of Women, and which derives from 2,000 years of struggle by women to assert themselves and claim what, from where I'm sitting, is a god-given birthright. When I was a girl, my choices in life if I wanted to work were three: a secretary, a schoolteacher, or a nurse. Fortunately, those days are over. But lest we get too complacent, here's a chilling fact: Women's wages *have remained more or less unchanged at one half to two thirds men's, since the seventeenth century.*

Here are two other divorce facts which will give you an overall quick sense of the situation and what's at stake:

1. In the year following a divorce the woman's standard of living falls by seventy-three percent, the man's rises by forty-two percent.
2. On a national level, a woman's income five years after divorce is thirty percent of what it was during the marriage. A man's income is fourteen percent higher.

The fight, it is clear, goes on.

CHAPTER

7

Going for 50%; The Process of
Taking a Divorce to Court

CHAPTER 7

HAVING DECIDED WE WERE GOING TO ASK FOR
fifty percent, we now had to prove why. My
lawyers already had from me a general outline of
the history of my marriage. But now we went into real detail
and left no stone unturned. I've talked at length about the all
important History of My Marriage, which more than any
other tool in the toolchest is useful for you both psychologically and legally.

In my case, with the lawyers we used that as a roadmap to
dwell on all those aspects of household maintenance which are
so often taken for granted, plus the way in which I shared with
him in all business decisions, acted as a sounding board, catalyst, and caretaker too. During the trial, when Robert's lawyer
tried to demean my contribution to the marriage, I responded
that it wouldn't have been any different if he'd been a baker or
an auto mechanic; I would have been right there alongside

him helping the dough rise and cleaning out the garage. I was an equal partner and stood behind the work I'd done on both his and our behalf.

It was clear to me that he wouldn't have been where he was without me.

A divorce has an orderly series of processes to it. First the case must be filed in the courtroom, and this filing must take place with both the parties present. I recall that I arrived first with my lawyers. The judge was not yet there. Finally Robert and his lawyer came in. In the eight months previous, Robert's and my contact had been limited to him asking me to come by to see the animals. I had thought this odd but had agreed to his request. So once a week, usually when I was out, he would come over to play with our cat and dog. Now he was sitting as quiet as a mouse on the bench. My lawyer went and talked a bit with his lawyer, then the judge came in and was presented with our papers. After this, we went into the judge's chambers, and the schedule of the trial was fixed.

The next phase of things takes place right after the filing of the case, when the court appoints you a list of five lawyers. From these, you must choose one to act as your mediator in the hopes—as I've mentioned already—that you settle out of court. My lawyers chose one of these five gentlemen, and not long after we duly assembled in his office, on a pouring, rainy evening.

I remember being in great spirits during this particular event and leaving the elevator for the conference room with all of us, Norman, Allan and myself, laughing hilariously. At a certain point, Norman said, Anyone seeing you just now would never believe you were going through a divorce. Is that what I'm going through? I said, because I'm having a hell of a time. We were still laughing as we entered the conference room, as I recall. Robert and his lawyers were sitting there, and Robert said, "Hi there, Vira." But Norman quickly short-circuited the conversation by stepping between us and ushering me to my seat. He was determined that we speak as little as possible. He believed it was bad for the case and could take us away from our focus.

Once seated, I watched the lawyers doing their badminton act back and forth, numbers flying through the air. I didn't take any of it too seriously, because I knew we were going to court. At a certain point of the evening, the lawyers gathered together in another room to attempt to hammer something out. After a half-hour, my lawyers returned and said nothing more than, "Vira, get your coat!" As we were walking away, they told me indignantly that Robert's side was offering less than ten percent. This was no surprise; I knew he was going to do something like that. What did surprise me was that as we got onto the elevator, a second later, before the doors could close, so did Robert and his lawyer.

In this atmosphere of awkward tension, no one said anything for a moment. Then, as the door was closing, I said politely to Robert and his lawyer, What floor are you fellows getting off on? This, of course, was a joke, given that we were all going together to the lobby. There was no answer to my question. "They're going to the top!" said Norman. I laughed out loud as Robert's eyes grew beady with anger. Stepping over to the comforting bulk of Norman, I held his arm.

The meeting from which we were all just then leaving had kicked off what's known as the mediation phase. If as a result of such mediation, there is still no settlement, you then move to a legal procedure called Deposition. This is a question and answer phase, in which the basic facts of the situation are fixed and recorded. The deposition takes place in both offices, those of the defendant and the plaintiff's lawyers. Each of you is asked questions about the marriage at length. Whatever material each lawyer has gathered on the case he or she now airs and probes with your help. You're under oath, the opponent is there, and the tension can grow pretty high. My reaction to this was typical: I totally ignored Robert. I absolutely removed him from my environment. He simply wasn't in my line of vision. And if he was, then I didn't see him. At the deposition he sat on one side with his lawyers, and I sat on the other. He might as well have been sitting in the middle of the Sahara desert. I was aiming at total concentration and clarity, attempting to be as honest and articulate in my thoughts as possible. To do that effectively, you have to eliminate whatever's around you. You must achieve perfect tunnel vision.

Robert was glowering at me the entire time, and I knew why: because not only was he giving me half of what he regarded as "his" fortune (he would say later he knew from the start I'd win, because "you don't fight with Vira"), but because I was going away! The woman who cooked and cleaned for him, the caretaker who cut his hair and charged his batteries—gone! I did feel sorry about that, because I knew he did really need me. But I also knew that we had come to the end of the road.

The deposition phase was concluded, but there was still, technically, the chance that the case would be settled out of court. Until one actually enters the courtroom with the trial judge presiding, there is always the chance of a settlement— often on the courtroom steps, as it turns out. But there was little possibility of that happening in my case, for the simple reason that first, as I said, Robert was offering only ten percent and was unwilling to go much higher, and second, I wanted to go to trial. That's right! I've always relished a good fight, especially when I had right on my side, and there was never a trial where there was a clearer case of right and wrong.

Since it was clear from early on that we couldn't reach a legal settlement, I got my wish, and a trial date was fixed.

Thus began the phase of "trial preparation." From my point of view, it was a continuing process of working away at the legal issues our team wanted to address. But there was another phase that involved me here, which I can't recommend enough to women in a similar situation. It had to do with being prepared as a witness.

Remember I said that a trial is a kind of theater, in which your team of actors (lawyers) has not only to present compelling analytic reasons for your case, but also "sway" the listeners, whether they be judge or jury.

It was my good fortune before my trial to work with Elaine Lewis. Elaine is an outstanding specialist in preparing witnesses for trial. She is also a wonderful student of human psychology and is able to keenly deduce your personality traits and your ability to project yourself in a public situation. She makes a quick study of you, your strengths and weaknesses, and then gives crucial coaching. Working with her gave me key guidance for how to act on the witness stand. As an added bonus, it was easy for me to see that Robert, during the trial, hadn't had the benefit of any coaching at all!

She began by posing endless questions, similar to those that might be thrown at me by a hostile lawyer. When I responded, she would dissect my answers, looking at the pros and cons. She studied me, how I behaved under pressure, how I typically answered a question, and what I could do to be a more effective witness.

She was very clear about the basics: I couldn't roll my eyes (a habit of mine). And most of all *I was not to get too animated under any circumstances.* The word given constantly to me was "flat," as in "keep it flat." Calm and relaxed, nonchalant but alert. And phrase my answers as precisely and accurately as I was able.

The opposing counsel would do his best to rattle me on the stand, because, in so doing, he would weaken the strength of my argument, which was that I was Robert's anchor, and his equal partner in the marriage. After all, if polished Robert Goldman was up on the stand politely answering questions in his courtly way, and his wife got up and revealed herself as volatile—a hothead—the judge would have no choice but to look at me as a person of diminished authority—to say the least.

So, as I say, ever-patient Elaine walked me through the trial, again and again. How I sat, the way I enunciated, the tone and timbre of the voice—all these things were worked and drilled. At moments I felt like my six-year-old self walking into my first music recital!

But as we'll see, my self-control and discipline were sorely tested during what all this homework and preparation were building toward: the trial.

Parents and Children;
Installing a Strong Base to Their Character;
Mothers and Daughters;
My Work as a Teacher

CHAPTER 8

ROBERT AND I WERE A TEAM, AS I'VE SAID, BOUND together by marriage and our desire to succeed. And yet, in our marriage as in every marriage, there were many compromises made in the interest of the common good. In my case, I subordinated my career aspirations to raise our daughter Olexa. I did this because it seemed the only appropriate thing to do. There is, of course, no "right" way to raise a child. Everyone does the best they can with the emotional and financial resources they have to hand. But based on my own experience, it seems to me that if a couple goes ahead and decides to have children, then they have a standing debt of responsibility to that helpless offspring—a debt which is not negotiable and must be paid in full if that child is to be a healthy, fulfilled, and successful adult. And if each partner pursues a booming public career without thought of the consequences for their child, then the child will suffer. This is not brain surgery; this is a simple law of nature.

I was an elementary education and art major in college, spent many years teaching kindergarten, and then, later in life, spent a lot of time around high-performance career-mad couples. I've always been sensitive to the influence of parental behavior on children, and I've watched from up close what happens in cases in which both parents are consumed by their careers. What happens is simple: as often as not the home life dries up and shrivels away, and the children are left to fend for themselves. They grow up helter-skelter, and they are forever emotionally altered by the experience. And usually not for the better. Nothing's writ in stone, of course, and children are incredibly adaptable. But parental absence during childhood is generally not a good thing. And babysitters, even excellent ones, are no replacement. I've always, by the way, thought it interesting that the advent of the chaotic "open classroom," heralded as a breakthrough in education but in fact adding more disorder and mismanagement to the teaching process, came into being at the very same time as the two-job marriage.

Children from unstable homes without the steadying influence of early parental attention typically show the symptoms of their insecurity by kindergarten. I've seen these children in my classes. They were frightened, stiff, aloof. They didn't "mix" easily, and often had a pale, worried look to them. To me it was deeply upsetting that children of age five were already bearing the signs of middle-age apprehension on their bright faces. They deserved better, and I often lavished attention on them, and in several cases managed to make them flower. I was especially sensitive to this, perhaps, because of the shattering effect on me of my mother leaving home to begin working when I was three. To this day I can divide my life into Before and After that watershed event. I believe that this is only natural: a young child is always attached to his or her mother, and it is through the mother that the first teachings and instructions about the ways of the world must always flow.

A sense of security in early life is the basis for the self-confidence that vaults children to the front of the class, and often, later in life, to the front of their chosen profession. And the sense of security in a young family comes from organization. Children require a routine, especially at an early age. If the child has to wonder each day, will dinner be at six or seven? Do I go to ballet class tonight? Can someone drive me to Little League? then that child is plunged abnormally early into adult anxieties and loses the stable foundation upon which one builds a secure, productive character.

So—I admit it—I ran my house like a friendly sergeant: I was organized and I kept to clear schedules. Obviously, once Olexa came bouncing into our life, I had to bend to accommodate her needs. Sometimes I felt I had to bend almost to the point of breaking. A child's world is a world of total dependence on you, and the transition from an independent adult to a mother with a helpless crying baby on her hands can cause a deep whiplash in your sense of self.

Ever the pragmatist, I bit the bullet and quickly organized my life and responsibilities around her requirements. Knowing that I had wanted a child very much and that there was a purpose and a goal to the demanding parts of childrearing made it much, much easier.

Robert and I lavished her with attention and gave her the fullest life we were capable of. He was not a doting dad—that wasn't his character—but he was an attentive father and cared deeply about her progress through life. And Olexa for her part was from the start a natural giver—a buoyant, generous soul who was the self-appointed den-mother of her friends. As she grew slowly into a cultured and attractive young woman, our pride and satisfaction kept pace alongside her.

The only time Robert became a little less than understanding was when she went through the magenta hair and black leather jacket phase of the American teen. He grew seriously riled, but I calmed him by asking: is she into drugs? No. Is she into promiscuous sex? No. Well, what are you worried about? Then there is no problem.

Actually, although he eventually took my point, I understood his concern. The fact is, it's almost impossible to remember one's childhood when you face it in your own child— almost impossible to remember how badly *you* once craved freedom, how impossibly square *your* parents seemed, and how you wished, just once, they could understand the agonies you were going through.

In the case of Olexa's punk phase, my question to Robert was: what harm is she really doing? As I say, he listened to it, and I'm glad he did, because if a child has a good base of self-worth already installed by his or her parents, then these kind of phases are just that—phases—which all children go through and out of which, like Olexa, they pass soon enough.

These periods of self-expression are extremely important in the life of a young teen. They are necessary to give them a preliminary sense of their independence and who they are in the wider world. So rather than squelch them because they make the parents uncomfortable, the parents should ride them out.

The truth is, many problems that parents have with these phases of their children's growth have less to do with the damage they might do to the children themselves or to society at large, and more on how they might reflect poorly on them, the parents. Rather than really looking at the issue and asking themselves: why is it happening? Is it healthy or not?, they look at it through the lens of who they are, and how society might see it, and this in turn derives from them not having enough confidence in themselves.

My message: whenever possible, trust your kids. If you've installed a good base to their character, then they should be able to ride out the occasional storms that blow through adolescence and growing up.

Mothers and Daughters

I'd like to talk in more detail about this relationship between mother and daughter, one of the most special, intuitive, potentially frustrating and deeply satisfying of all relationships in the world. It begins with the moment in which this helpless infant returns with you from the hospital.

From that moment on, what was once your house, the place you and your husband lived in quite happily, is now after a fashion, Her house. You open the front door, and holding her tight in your arms, you introduce her to her new life. You bring her into her new room, a room that you've spent many loving hours to decorate.

In the nine months you've had to plan for this new arrival, you've prepared a comfortable space. Perhaps you've repainted the walls a warm color. Maybe you've hung fabric. You've gone out and bought the little bassinet, the swaddling cloths and clothing. Friends have showered you with baby toys, and you've been inundated with gifts as well.

Of course, well before the homecoming moment, you were thinking about the awesome responsibility that lay ahead of you as a parent. From the moment your pregnancy was announced, you began, on some level, to take life differently. You started to think of yourself as a mother, with a mother's responsibilities. You began to prepare for the challenges and rewards of your new life through constant reading, and endless conversations with your friends.

In my case, as I recall, it was the dead of winter when we brought our daughter home from the hospital. Snow was heaped high, and the streets were silent. This was in the town of Irvington on Hudson, New York. In the distance, the Hudson River lay grey and still. The white snow fell against the sunny sky, with white clouds surrounding us, and we looked at our precious gift, her soft, pink skin wrapped in a pink cotton gown, and we felt secure and complete. We knew that our own lives would never quite be the same.

My own experience was that as deeply independent as I was by nature, I found my entire life bent around my child. She instantly became the center of all the things in my world that mattered. Whatever duties my day consisted of, they all, in some manner, referred back to her. I recall that I had a health problem around that time, and that the cold breath of fear blew over me—not for what might have happened to me, but because of what it would have meant for her to be raised without a mother.

The mother's relationship with the child is among life's deepest, most fierce, and instinctual. It is a sacred trust and a joy.

Growth and Separation

From the moment the newborn sits up, begins to look around, take in the world around her, and attempts to speak, you're off and running on a new phase in your lifelong collaboration. It's in fact about childrearing that I'd like to speak now. We all know that it's a natural tendency to raise the child in our own likeness. The child comes from us, after all. And herein lies the difficulty. Our maternal instincts move us to help and love and care for the child, but they also allow us occasionally to forget that this child, though it is derived from us, is still an individual, with a separate will and a separate destiny. The only way to achieve this understanding is by separating emotionally from your child, and learning to live outside their frame, looking in. You are there, you are listening, you are alert, but you do not intrude until it becomes apparent that your presence is required.

If the child is a girl, in addition to the love and tenderness there is also, as the child grows, a kind of wary instinct she develops toward her mother, the better to achieve her own independence. There is a portion of automatic difficulty in the relationship, not planned or intentional, but there nonetheless. The daughter loves the mother as life-giver, as teacher, protector, consoler and guide. But in that guidance is also the potential for a war of wills when that control becomes controlling, when those various demands become demanding. The daughter looks at the mother and says to herself, "She always thinks she knows best, just because she's older and my parent. But if she only knew how I felt."

The mother looks at the daughter and says to herself, "I wish she would understand that I am only looking out for her best interests, that she grow and develop to the best in accordance with her god-given talents and develop that inner light of spirituality that is her human side. I wish she would understand I desire only to nourish and protect her against the outside elements of the world, so that no harm comes to her."

These mother's emotions are, of course, most strongly felt during the early period of raising a child, in which the main responsibilities are to love and nurture, that period in which the child is growing by incredible amounts each day, learning through the senses the world around her, and requiring the elemental comforts of warmth and security and a full stomach, of being caressed, swaddled, and kept happy. This is a sensitive little object! And the dependence on the mother at this phase is total.

Of course, what people may not realize as clearly is that at the same time the mother nurtures the child she is, after a fashion, nurturing herself, and contributing to her own spiritual growth. She may be too bound round with diapers and teething rings to notice, but she is actually undergoing an enriching experience, one of the fundamental enriching experiences which life can bestow on us!

There has never been a perfect parent, nor a perfect child, of course. But my philosophy has always been that the worst thing a mom can do is harp, peppering the child with do's and don'ts. My thought is: save the little don'ts for the Big Don't and choose your battles carefully. If you harp and become a harper, that child is not going to pay much attention to you at the crucial moment in time when you want to sit down and talk about some of the big and serious things in life. They will have grown habituated to a negative emotional climate from their years as toddlers, and will have already turned off.

A case in point. For many years I was dying to tell my daughter what to do about a specific thing that was troubling her. I was certain I knew exactly what to do. But I held my fire, as hard as it might have been. When she finally came around on her own to make the decision I'd been praying for, she was happy at her achievement and came to me with love in her heart.

Sometimes the hardest thing in the world for a mother to do is to maintain that hand's-off posture as regards her own child. Having become used to sweeping into situations and setting them right, it can be agonizing to hold off, sit back, and watch your child stumble and bark her shins on the sills of life before slowly growing into a new understanding. But it is absolutely essential that you let the child do this, that you allow her to build her own muscle and that you don't overcrowd and over mother her. After you give birth, you have to look at this child as if she came not only from you, but from some other place. Imagine her as a stranger, a wrinkled cute little stranger, come to you from afar.

As to the children themselves, I think we can break their development down into a series of leaps and plateau states, jumps upwards of incredibly fast growth followed by periods of slower growth, in which they consolidate the gains they've made. Take kindergarten. Kindergarten, for children, is the New World, a place stranger than anything they've ever experienced before. They jump from the entirely warm and familiar nest of the home to the bleak truth of Other People. They are no longer among familiar adults cuffing them under the chin and admiring them for their cute good looks, but among their peers. They are learning to deal on a one-to-one basis in kindergarten—eyeball to eyeball with their coevals. They must resolve whatever issues come up amongst themselves. Here we can usually glimpse the first real stirrings of independence.

But children are also very resilient, and most of them make it past this hurdle with only a few bumps. The next big hurdle, of course, is adolescence, which is a very big hurdle indeed. All those hormones come crashing into the unsuspecting body, and this body suddenly becomes aware of itself, and of other bodies. At adolescence, for the first time, you look outside yourself and take a measure of the society around you. You're entering high school, beginning to date. The social pressures are enormous. They cause the repeated questioning of the self: who am I? How am I different from the others?

Unfortunately, as regards the mother in this period, it's a very difficult time. She now assumes a role which, for all intents and purposes, is that of the warden. She buries her child with "don'ts." Her mothering suddenly seems for the most part to reside in placing limits on her daughter. You have to be home by eleven! No, you can't wear that skirt! To the daughter, of course, all this appears absurd, or worse than absurd, nearly criminal. The mother whom she trusted with her deepest confidences has suddenly transformed herself into an ogre, a monster, whose sole goal in life is to fence in her daughter.

All of this, of course, changes drastically when the child becomes a mother herself. When she gives birth, she has a revelation of sorts and the wheel comes full circle, and she begins the process of searching out *her* mother. This can be a literal looking for her mother, or an emotional quest to come to terms with her mother's influence, but it's always a process of drawing closer in spirit. The daughter, at this phase, becomes deeply curious to know the whys of her own mothering. Mom, what did you do when I did X? What did you do when I did Y, or when any of a hundred issues and problems arose? The daughter draws near; the pendulum shifts, and the mother who you were pushing away for so many years suddenly—miraculously!—turns into a fountain of crucial information about raising children.

My relationship with my own mother was quite different from my relationship with my daughter. My mother, as I've already explained, came from a peasant village in remote Ukraine, a farmer's daughter in a very very poor environment, where the tough daily duties—and large families—tended to work against the more fine-scale intimacies. She was a woman of limited education and enormous natural gifts.

On top of that, she happened to grow up amidst a historical situation of enormous difficulty, with bombs dropping around her and the madness of the First World War exploding in her young girlhood. These things change you. They make you tough where we are tender. The life of my own mother is something my daughter, paging through a book or watching a movie, might see depicted.

My daughter's environment, of course, was one of relative affluence. She grew up in or near the most cosmopolitan city in the world, exposed by her parents to everything life had to offer. In the kind of upward mobility in which America specializes, the women of my family moved in three generations from a tiny Ukrainian village to a position of incredible privilege. I love America for so many things—for its democratic institutions, its liberty, its strength, and most of all for its people. It's been good to me and my family, and the arc from my mother's birth in a hardscrabble Ukrainian village to the life of access, education and comfort of my daughter is a perfectly realized example of the American dream.

Teaching and Thomas

I've mentioned before that I was a teacher. I'd like to conclude this chapter by speaking a moment about the crucial ways in which the roles of teaching and parenting in life are similar. Both of them, after all, have as their goal the installing of a stable base in a child's character. And both, though they have many dutiful responsibilities attached, are far, far more than just a job. Speaking from my own experience, I can say that for me to take a young mind full of pure potential, and open that mind to the joy of learning, has produced some of the deepest satisfaction I've known. Though as mentioned I had to give up teaching when my own child came, I continued tutoring, and substitute teaching, and this was important to me too. My specialty as a tutor was dyslexia, and having been there myself, and suffering from dyslexia, I worked well with a variety of children. For some reason, when I think back over that time of my life, I find my thoughts dwelling on a little boy named Thomas.

I met Thomas one afternoon while subbing at the local school. Walking down the hallway, I saw a child standing there outside of the classroom, after having been obviously kicked out of class by the teacher. He was a rough, scruffy little kid who was wearing a deeply unhappy look on his face.

"Aren't you standing on the wrong side of the door?" I asked him.

He stuck out his lower lip and said, "The teacher said I'm not behaving in class, so she sent me out into the hall."

Something about the boy, some sense I had, prompted me to look past the slightly street-kid exterior and see the diamond in the rough. I called his mother that night. Yes, she admitted, he's having study problems, and we hear he's acting out in class too. On the spot, I offered to tutor him. I liked Thomas, but more than that I had a sneaking suspicion he might be dyslexic, and I was curious to put my hunch to the test. Sure enough, at our very first meeting, I found my suspicions confirmed. Not only was Thomas dyslexic, but he was suffering from the classic side effect of a reading difficulty: lack of self-esteem.

As with all the students I tutored, my first challenge was to build him up. I did this through my tried and true method: by finding out what was the one thing in the world he was best at. In Thomas's case, it was taking apart and reassembling mechanical objects. He was a positive whiz at breaking down and putting together clocks and bicycles. This, I realized, was my opening, and I took it. Thomas, I said, do you know that if we went into your classroom, and even the classroom of the grade higher than yours, I'm almost 100 percent sure we couldn't find a better dismantler than you? Really? he asked, open-mouthed with surprise.

Yes, I told him. Oh, sure, they may be better readers, but there's no one in those classes who can handle springs and gears and cogs like you do. I guarantee it!

Thomas rewarded me for this with a big smile. I could tell that the dam had been broken. And from that moment on, we were off and running. Little by little I was able to repair his self-esteem, and with that convince him to reinsert himself into the social frame of his class. He began to try to follow the lessons, with the result that his grades began steadily to rise. To this day I look back on Thomas as one of my most satisfying success stories, and symbolic of a whole series of children who I helped over the hurdles of learning to read.

CHAPTER

9

The Trial; The Importance of Preparation;
Keeping a Cool Head on the Stand

CHAPTER 9

THE DAY OF DECEMBER 15, 1997 DAWNED BRIGHT and sunny. Most of New York went about its day that particular morning the way it always did. But in a small, low-ceilinged courtroom on Center Street in lower Manhattan, my future personal history, and with it a chunk of American legal precedent, was about to be decided. My lawyers and I sat at our table, eagerly awaiting the entrance of the judge and the start of the day's events. Over the course of the pre-trial proceedings, we had the good fortune to avoid most disputes over pre-trial disclosure of financial information and thereby advance the case more speedily toward the trial itself. We wanted the trial for a variety of reasons, as I've explained, but one among them was that Robert was using "my money" to draw up his case, even though it was "marital funds" that he controlled. He, after all, was the "have," and I was the "have not."

We were feeling quite confident, but we were also slightly concerned by the fact that none of us really knew Judge Tolub. Obviously, if one of your lawyers already has a working relationship or a history of some kind with a judge, you can already begin making deductions based on that history. But about Judge Tolub we knew nothing, save that he had a reputation for being a straight shooter and had a minimum tolerance for nonsense in his courtroom—he moved things along and liked to keep a tight schedule.

The judge entered and seated himself. My very first reaction was a simple one: "Omigod, the judge's desk and chair are so high I can't see him!" Inwardly, I thought, wait, if I can't see him, how can I know what he's hearing? Is he hearing every word? I didn't want him to miss a thing, after all, but what if he couldn't see the participants? What if he goes to sleep up there? Actually, he's a giant of a judge, and he ruled with the wisdom of a Moses in my case. But at the time, my reaction was, oh no, what am I going to do?

As trials do, this trial began officially with the opening statements of the lawyers. Robert's lawyer, Larry Pollack, stood up first and made his. He was a short, balding man who always looked like he could use a good night's sleep, and I already had a negative impression of him from an exchange of letters which, on his part, seemed to me to be poorly written. As I listened to him speak, I felt my suspicions about him confirmed. Below all the rhetoric and legal terminology, his argument struck me as chauvinistic, simplistic and wrong-headed. It boiled down to this: that basically I didn't need all the money. Yes, legally I was entitled, of course, but according to his line of reasoning, I had already had enough.

My reaction was: who is he to tell me how much I need and how much I don't need? What gives him the authority and the power to determine that? It was his job to say this, and he was doing that job perfectly. I was not angry, per se, because to my thinking, in the world of justice and truth, Larry Pollack's statement simply *didn't fit*. He knew nothing about where I came from, about what I'd done with my life and marriage, and in that context, his approach was so off the mark as to be ridiculous. Norman, in any case, stood up and quickly flipped the sense out of his argument, by saying, "why is the *he* part more important than the *she* part, when both partners worked equally as hard towards the same goal?" Norman correctly underlined the patronizing side of Pollack's argument, which in essence ran: "let's give the dear little woman enough to live on, and she'll be fine."

I was pleased to see, right away, that Norman's point was hitting home to the judge. There was no obvious sign of this; I could just tell. But then again I was feeling pretty confident in general. From a legal point of view we had done all our homework and were totally prepared. On top of this I had deep inner confidence that I was in the right, and that all I had to do was explain to the judge exactly what I'd brought to my marriage for him to see my side of the picture. The truth is, I never had a moment of doubt that I wouldn't come out on top, no matter what the opposition said.

After a little more opening folderol, Robert was called to the witness stand. He got to his feet. I watched him with complete detachment. Often in such cases as these, at the end of a long marriage, there is a lot of sentiment: scenes of heartbreak, tears, and regrets. None of that in my case! I've always had the ability to detach and look at things unsentimentally. Also, as importantly, it was I who wanted to bring things to an end. Mainly what I felt was sorry for him, because I knew that by leaving him I was making his life enormously difficult. But there was nothing I could do anymore, and he would have to find his own way in life. For me, at this particular moment, it was merely another problem to deal with. I had no time to allow myself to sit down and feel sorry.

Robert sat in the witness stand, as impeccably tailored and distinguished-looking as ever. And yet, I saw him already as if from the far side of a perception—as another person who I had to get through to get on with my life. I wanted truth and fairness between us. We had had a good marriage, but it was over. I had no hatred of the man. I simply wanted our worldly goods divided equally, nothing more, nothing less.

He continued testifying in his low, courteous voice, being led by his lawyer through prearranged questions. There was much discussion of intricate financial details. But Robert's main point seemed to be, "we think she was wonderful and terrific, but we're not going to give her fifty percent." One of their strategies to accomplish this was to try to play down my contribution to the social side of marriage, and show that I'd had a less than decisive role in the business side of our private life, i.e. had done less than my share as a corporate wife. This didn't wash, because the truth was that I had always been there, socially, whenever he requested it. I had cooked for many business functions, and attended most if not all of the dinner parties among business associates. I was very outgoing and social by nature, and Robert was retiring. So, yet another of Pollack's ploys was shot down.

As I've already said, I've always loved a good scrap, and I think I'll probably come back as a litigating lawyer in the next life. The trial exhilarated me. I loved every part of it. Early on, I'd loved the research to build the case, the long process of bringing the honest facts to light and assembling them, the digging and shaping, the arriving at clarity finally, and then the march into the courtroom, ready to argue, deduce and convince. To me this was extremely exciting. I had a righteous cause and truth on my side. To present that truth and convince other people to see what I saw was thrilling to me.

The only other time I'd felt this particular sense of challenge and adventure had been in my days as a teacher, where I knew the same excitement in a successful classroom situation. When teaching and preparing elementary school children, you've got clear objectives. You want to get knowledge across to the children, impart information for them to understand and digest. Your hope is that they'll be as excited about it as you are, turn the information around and present it back to you as something of their own. That moment of illumination in a child is what you're after. The end result, of course, is the great satisfaction that *they* have, in having given back to you. Look, they say, what I have produced out of what you fed me. That turnaround of information, that imparting of your excitement and point of view to another, is the true joy of teaching. In a courtroom, when this same thing happens, there is a word for it. It's called *winning*.

As the case went on, his lawyer began to seem to me more and more wrong-headed. And then there was the "boomerang" factor, as I called it. Boomerangs was my word for Robert's various legal strategies, which invariably, it seemed, would come back and hit him on the head. One after another, the witnesses for Robert would troop up to the stand and give testimony that was either flat, unconvincing, or in some cases outright damaging to his case.

Take Robert's attempt to establish through "expert testimony" that a substantial part of our fortune—the shares of Congress itself—was his "separate" property and thereby deny me rights to it. He attempted to do this in two ways. First, he hired an expert to trace the origins of the Congress shares in the hope that he could demonstrate that a large segment were purchased or owned by his family prior to the marriage and that he'd been "gifted" his shares in the business. Although Robert and his expert put a great deal of effort into this endeavor—a report, for example, was issued by the expert declaring a large portion of the stock to be Robert's "separate" property—they were really tilting at windmills. The undisputed documentary evidence showed that Robert had purchased his shares from his father and other family members and had received a large share of his holdings as compensation from Congress during his marriage to me. Through skillful analysis on the acquisition of Robert's holdings that we'd prepared as documentary evidence, Norman handily demolished Robert's expert on the stand during the trial.

Robert's other main argument for reducing the "marital" portion of the Congress shares that were subject to distribution to me was that he had acquired his interest in the business before the marriage and that much of the increased value of the shares was "passive," i.e. not the result of his (or my) efforts. The clear implication of this was that the huge success of Congress had nothing to do with Robert himself, even though he'd been at the helm the entire time.

Once again, cross examination at the trial of Robert's expert (this time by Allan) effectively eliminated Robert's claim of separate property. The hired expert, in fact, knew nothing of the particular facts of the Goldmann's case. He had not met Robert and was unaware of what efforts Robert had made on behalf of the company. Most importantly, he had ignored the fact that, even when stock market indicators rise, each company succeeds or fails on the efforts of its individual management. Congress, in otherwords, could not simply ride the tide of a generally rising stock market and assume success without appropriate decision-making by management—led by none other than Robert.

Ironically enough, the bankruptcy filing of The Wiz had just taken place, a fact noted by the judge, who threw out all of Robert's "separate" property arguments.

Finally it was my turn to testify. I felt very cool and composed on the witness stand. Although inwardly very alert, I was outwardly quite calm. During the cross-examination by Larry Pollack, I kept coming back with strength and confidence. "Larry," I said, "I lived with Robert Goldman for thirty-three years, and you're making it sound like he was the employer and I the employee. It's not "his" money—that's the point, it's "our" money." Larry, I wanted to say, it's called the twentieth century. Read about it!

But he kept right on going, describing our net worth as "his," instead of ours and relegating me to the position of upstairs maid.

All this I was prepared for and could deal with. I was prepared for the negative aspersions that would be cast on my character and the innuendoes that would be bandied about during the trial. It rolled right off me like water off a duck's back. The only time I almost lost my self-control was when Larry Pollack began drilling at me with repetitive questions about Congress Factors and ALLLLL that money. He was trying to set me up as a venal schemer who had been after Robert Goldman's money all the way from day one, when neither of us had any. I saw this coming, and I headed him off by saying, "It did not matter what Robert Goldman did. I would have done the exact same things in this life if my husband had been a butcher or baker instead of a businessman. If he had been a baker and said to me, "OK, we have to get the dough to rise, or OK, we have to mop the floor, I would have been fine with that. Whatever he did, I wanted him to do it to the best of his ability, and I was there to help him do just that, day in, day out, for thirty-three years."

Me saying this had the effect of diverting Pollack from his character assassination and bringing him down to the world of reality. Nonetheless, the slow repetitiveness of the questions irritated me. I felt like I was sitting up there being tormented by a big, slow-moving bumblebee that I was forbidden to swat away!

I've never been one to hide my feelings, and I guess it became obvious I was beginning to get furious. The questions continued, and as they did my eye fell on the bible sitting in front of me. I stared at it, wondering, if I pick this up and fling it across the room, can I hit him right between the eyes? Across the room, Norman and Allan were holding their breath. They knew what I was going through. They were beaming me silent messages: hold on, Vira! Keep it flat! Don't let go! Meanwhile, the wandering, irrelevant questions continued. Bzz Bzz buzzed the bumblebee! I could feel my rage mounting. But I succeeded in controlling myself and retaining my composure. The questioning eventually stopped, and I stepped down.

Their very last witness was called, and in a certain sense was a perfect symbol of their ineffectual trial strategy. He was an old friend who was supposed to prove something about Robert's finances. But this man on the stand proved to have no important recollections supporting Robert's case, and then came the kicker: after leaving the witness box, this supposedly "hostile" witness came directly over to me, leaned over, took my hands, and hugged them to his chest, and, looking in my eyes, said "How good it is to see you," and then kissed me on the cheek. The entire courtroom went into a state of shock! And the trial was over. Now it remained only to sit and await the verdict.

CHAPTER

10

The Role of Women in the World;
Changing Social Values;
The Family Unit Under Seige

CHAPTER 10

WHAT WOULD THE JUDGE BE CONSIDERING AS he came to his verdict? He would be considering the strength of our arguments, he would be considering the specifics of our marriage and the relative contributions each of us made, and he would be doing this in the context of our present day society. My hope was that he would understand that way in which today's society so often plays the game of a double standard with women, assigning them crucial responsibilities, and then often undervaluing those same responsibilities. Society, for example, seems to imply that women must choose between career and family —as if having a family isn't a career in and of itself!

If anything, home, marriage, and the raising of children is more than one career; it's several careers rolled into one. The job of mothering a child is never-ending. Add to that dealing with the husband, and taking care of HIS psyche, and add to that some professional work in the world, and you have a very full dance card.

The judge was a mature, middle-aged man, and he therefore came from the time when a man traditionally went out into the world, and he made changes in that world. He played on a bigger field than his wife. He ruled countries, ran powerful corporations. But the judge would also surely know that this rigid division of roles is changing, and he would also, I hoped, realize that no matter how high-flying and globe-trotting a man is, he requires the same creaturely and emotional comforts as any human, and needs a private space where he can rejuvenate himself and rest. Without this space, he would quickly lose his taste for those public battles which bring him such glory as a man.

Many things in life are complex, but when two people come together and they decide they want to spend the rest of their days together, they have a simple question they should put to themselves: what are our goals? Once they establish those goals, they should try to determine how best to obtain them. The important thing in a marriage is not who does what, but that together, in whatever form you desire or have evolved, you reach your goals. Who's to say then that one role is less important than the other? Who's to say that building a nest and keeping it functioning—and an infinite amount of things go into that—isn't the equal of banking or finance or being an auto mechanic for that matter? In a long-term marriage, couples tend to each take on a variety of roles not easily defined but nonetheless crucial to the health of the family. If that same couple reaches its goals in life, and then decides for whatever reasons to split up, who's to say that this interwoven web of duties known as "marriage" can be easily split into the "HIS AND HERS?"

I'm sorry, but that's not the way it works.

Unfortunately, society has evolved in such a way as to judge the role of the wife and mother somehow "inferior," or "less important" than that of the professional who is outside the home. Now just think, if women one day said, "That's it, I'm not going to be a wife or a mother. I'm not going to build a nest or raise children. No, I'm just going to go out into the world and "do my thing," and develop my career, and that's all there is to it." How long would society last then before falling to pieces?

The perpetuation of the species is not exactly a side-job, excuse me! And yet, over the years, the idea of being in the home became itself viewed as something disrespectful. Being a businesswoman or a professional became the end-all and be-all, and work outside the home, for magical reasons, became somehow more "prestigious," more "valuable." What I'd like to ask is, more valuable to whom?

The answer is easy: to men. It's their fault that the woman has historically been treated as an inherently lesser person in her relationship with her mate, and under these circumstances, it makes perfect sense that a woman would say to herself, OK, for me to be considered an equal, I must go outside the home, enter the rough and tumble world of business and prove myself. The rub in all this, of course, is that she has less time and energy for her family in general, and for her children specifically.

And the children are the point.

I'm all for women's emancipation, and consider myself first and foremost an emancipated woman. We can't go backward in anyway who would want a return to the way things were, vis a vis men and women? Not I! But I don't think, for the child's sake, that we can eliminate the family unit either.

The family unit is under attack these days. Women, due to artificial insemination, can now have children by themselves and raise them with or without a father. Men are now an option—unthinkable in my generation! Be that as it may, what I'm asking for here is a return to a focus on the family, and a *sharing* of the time between career and home. The math is simple: there are only so many hours in a day, and you can't be a "total" career woman and be totally a part of your home life at the same time. Yes, if you can afford to, you may hire nannies and can say happily to yourself that "at least the child is being looked after; the house is kept neat and clean." But that's not the point. We're not talking about an efficient or well-functioning household, though both those things are important. We're talking about the emotional center, the great warm light at the heart of a family that comes from a mother's love and attention.

Ask yourself: is the average child going to connect to a babysitter or nanny the way that child connects to the woman from whose body it's been born? Continuity is key to the building of a stable young character. When a child leaves school at the end of the day and returns home bursting to tell of those hundred tiny things that happened that day, it's essential that child have his mother in front of him. A nanny or babysitter do not quite fit the bill. With hired help, as good as they may be, there's a gap, a lack, an emptiness at the core. The fact of the matter is that being there, day in, day out, for as much and often as possible, particularly in the early years, is crucial to a child's development. There's a connection between child and mother entirely different from child and father. The umbilical cord, though it's cut at birth, continues symbolically for awhile. The psyche of the child is inherently constructed so as to relate, at least at the beginning, to the person feeding it—the warmth and pressure and familiar sound and smell of the mother. Certainly there can and should be help for the mother (though I had none), but the mother is the main figure, and as such the main giver of security, confidence and strength to a child. The mother is the natural support system, and if that maternal connection is severed, the child starts out life at a disadvantage, removed from a whole range of emotional possibilities.

These points are important and bear repeating. I'm not pushing for a black and white withdrawal of women from society. Far from it! I'm only suggesting an emphasis, a placement of energy on the child, particularly during the first years of life. Those first few years of life host one of the most incredible growth spurts in all of nature. During that phase of a child's development, every day brings an entire new universe of possibilities to life. Babies go from lying flat on their backs, to sitting upright, to crawling, toddling, and walking and then running—all within a phenomenally short space of time.

When a young, career-minded woman with a baby, intoxicated with the bright lights of her professional promise, ends up spending most of her life out of the home, she often rationalizes it away by saying to herself that somewhere later along the line she'll recapture the phases her child is going through; she'll make it up. A word to the wise: it doesn't work like that. There *is* no going back. You can't make up later for what you didn't give at first. The child is growing at lightning speed during the early years, and he or she needs you then most of all, day in, day out.

Some mothers who feel they must give the time over to their careers take the route of placing children in day-care centers. Obviously, if economic necessity dictates it, that's one thing, but to remove the baby forcibly from its nest and environment, and warehouse it in a cave with two or three other women and a bunch of screaming children, seems to me a less-than-ideal solution if there are alternatives. People think, it's only a baby, what does it know? I have news for them: it knows quite a lot. The baby can't reason intellectually, but the senses are highly attuned. The baby has an intuitive sense when it's comfortable and amidst familiar surroundings, and when not. The baby in its own secure environment with its own mother knows it well. And among the things it knows is when it's being taken away from home and away from all that!

As I mentioned earlier, I have been a hard-working woman my whole life and am descended from a long-line of hard-working women. When I decided to have a child, I said to myself, I know I will have to make sacrifices to do it. But I don't want to burn myself alive either, and give myself up ENTIRELY to home, husband and child. So I did what I would advise other women in my circumstances to do, if they can possibly afford it: compromise. Yes, that's right. Work at a reduced intensity, and tailor that work to the important rhythms of your child's and family's life. There are ways to find the time in a day to do that for yourself, if you're organized. Let's say for example my profession is accounting. Obviously, if I'm concerned about the welfare of my family and young child, I can't work a 9-5 job, but I CAN do it on the side, keeping my thumb in, staying active and keeping my professional credentials up to date for that moment later in time when I can fully enter into my profession.

It's a matter of emphasis, of clear-headed investment of time and energy in such a way as to have both a private and a professional life. Clearly, the kind of time-sharing logic I'm talking about here doesn't apply to every job. If you're a doctor, you have an around-the- clock commitment to your work. But my point is that you *can* parcel out your time wisely and do it in a way so that it has as gentle an impact as possible on your family life.

It's important to remember that life is long, that people live to much more of an advanced age than they used to, and that later on, at a point in time when the child is less reliant on you, you can always pick up your job with renewed energy and vigor. And each year after a certain age—usually somewhere around five—you'll have a little bit more time to yourself.

Privileging the home life as I recommend does not take away; it adds. You have two jobs—actually many more than two jobs; but in the main, two jobs. Motherhood should be valorized by the culture; motherhood and the administering of a household should be prized for what they are: the pillars of our society, nothing less.

CHAPTER
11

*The History of Women's Rights in America;
Getting the Vote;
Women's Finances Today*

CHAPTER 11

I WAITED WHILE THE JUDGE WENT ABOUT HIS BUSINESS of deciding the verdict. I knew he would have a mountain of paperwork to sift through—my legal team had left no stone unturned, after all, and we had brought thousands of pages of documents to the trial to back up our claims. I had other projects to take up my time just then and remained confident and productive. And I hoped as the judge reasoned and analyzed within himself that he would take a moment to reflect on the history of women's rights in America of which his verdict might be a small but still not insignificant part.

The history of women's rights in America is, of course, directly related to the history of women's work in America. It shouldn't surprise us that in the early Colonial period that work was almost entirely connected to the home and family. Women labored long, back-breaking hours in the fields. They tended the cattle, raised the children, spun the wool which they made into bedding and clothing, and were also usually responsible for household items like soap, candles, and medicines. When they went outside the home to make a living, they usually did so by resorting to one of two jobs: being a seamstress, or running a boardinghouse. Yes, a small percentage of them became teachers, doctors, lawyers and other professionals too, but by the early nineteeth century, acceptable occupations for women were by and large limited to factory labor or domestic work. At-home nursing was considered an appropriate job for women, but in hospitals, it was still male nurses who held sway.

On the one hand, social pressures kept women out of the higher professions. It was considered "unwomanly" to do many of the things we take for granted today. It was considered "beneath" women to work late, or lift heavy objects. But there was also the force of law behind these beliefs. Women, for example, were not only discouraged from attending medical school—a woman doctor seemed to most nineteenth-century men something like a two- headed horse—they were also outright forbidden. And if they tried to flout the law and get an education by attending school, they were arrested and thrown in jail.

The Industrial Revolution sent women wholesale out of the home and into factories, changing the family structure forever, and beginning the long struggle for equal pay for equal labor. But the American woman's struggle to be paid the same as men—a struggle still underway in fact—was only a strand in that larger tapestry that has been an interest of American women from the very first: Reform.

Perhaps it was because they were involved in raising children and were always looking to improve things for their offspring that American women, from the start, were deeply involved in banding together to work at improving the society around them. Women in this country spearheaded the drive to ban alcohol from the home, improve education (many women were teachers, almost from the first), and better working conditions in factories. Women were in the forefront of trying to make prisons livable and worked hard to found many of the abolitionist movements to free the slaves. (These women were of course moved by the plight of imprisoned Africans. But slavery was also the way many frustrated nineteenth-century American women saw themselves as wives, which lent their abolitionist efforts a special force). They worked to send missionaries to the Indians and to provide housing and food for widows and orphans.

It was in the late-nineteenth century that women began to band together to try to throw off the legal and social fetters that they felt bound them. The "suffrage" movement was founded, and in 1895 Elizabeth Cady Stanton published a huge bestseller called *The Woman's Bible*, which, among other things, created a giant scandal when it criticized church authority and attacked the use of Scripture to promote woman's subjugation. Ministers attacked this "godless" book and tried to stem the liberalizing tide, but their efforts were doomed. American women had a new goal, and they were going to fight until they got it: that goal was to achieve the vote.

The Vote

American women were the first in the world to organize themselves to demand the vote. But well before they'd gotten organized, they were already working on an individual basis to con-

vince the government to let them have this precious democratic right. These demands began all the way back at the
beginning. The *very* beginning. In 1647, an ambitious woman
named Margaret Brent tried to get the right to vote in
Baltimore and was denied it. Through the 1700s, women
would sporadically demand to be counted, only to be rejected
by the authorities. It would be in the nineteenth century that
women's efforts to achieve the vote would really gather steam.
Women who were already involved in working against slavery
banded together in the 1850s to use their newfound political
clout to begin agitating for the vote. In the words of Elizabeth
Cady Stanton, "it is the duty of women in this country to
secure themselves their sacred right to the franchise."

It was a "duty" that was not easily granted by the men who
ran the country. When it came to reasons for denying women
the vote, men proved to be remarkably resourceful. One of the
most common reasons given was that women were "hysterical"
and incapable of making a rational choice. There was also the
idea that women were inherently dependent on men and sub-
ordinate to them and therefore would be unable to exercise the
independence of mind necessary to choose. Priests and ministers thundered predictably that women should confine their
influences to the home. More practically, the liquor, brew, and
textile companies (many women worked killingly long hours
in the mills) were afraid that giving women the vote would
mean legislation damaging to their businesses.

But women persevered.

Susan B. Anthony, the pride of my hometown of
Rochester, was a great and tireless fighter for women's rights.
She was a Quaker who came out of the temperance movement

determined to make women's votes count. Along with Elizabeth Cady Stanton, she founded the American Equal Rights Association, and in 1868, they started publishing the newspaper *The Revolution* in Rochester, with the masthead "Men their rights, and nothing more; women, their rights, and nothing less," and the aim of establishing "justice for all."

It's a very worthy idea.

In the early-twentieth century, the right-to-vote movement really began to pick up speed, and for good reason: educated, middle-class women looked around and asked themselves the question: why is it that I can't vote, when immigrant men, many of them illiterate, poorly educated and barely speaking English, can, and therefore have the legal right to decide my future?

In 1918, militant suffragists chained themselves to the White House fence. And finally, in 1919, an American congress, grateful for women's crucial contributions during World War I, passed a constitutional amendment granting women the vote. It was ratified by the states the very next year.

But it would not be so simple as enacting some new laws. Yes, women had the vote, but below that were deep-seated cultural attitudes that change about as fast as a glacier melts. Take today. It's now been forty years since the Equal Pay Act was passed in 1963, and guess what? American women working full-time still *earn an average of seventy-four cents for each dollar earned by men*, according to a new report. Interestingly enough, the pay gap stays the same even if men and women work at the same job for a long time. Women engineers with the same qualifications as men can grow old in their jobs and never close the salary difference (which is about twenty-six percent). Yet another study found that women physicians earned less than men in forty-four of forty-five specialties, including obstetrics-gynecology (fourteen percent less) and pediatrics (15.8 percent less.)

So women make less than men do when they do men's jobs. Not all that surprising, perhaps. But what about *women's* jobs? Well, part of the problem is that the jobs that are traditionally held by women are themselves undervalued by the culture at large. That's because the "culture at large," with its government, its financial institutions, its legal establishment, is all mainly run by men. And so, despite all the noise about feminism these last few decades, more than 55 percent of employed women still work in traditional "women's jobs"—librarians, clerical workers, nurses, teachers, and child care workers. These jobs pay a lot less—and for no good reason! I ask you: is a truck driver—who earns an average annual wage of $30,000—really forty-five percent more valuable than a child care worker who may have a four-year degree in early childhood education and who is responsible for overseeing a helpless human life? Is a beginning engineer really worth between thirty and seventy percent more than a beginning teacher, if both have the same grad-school training?

It comes down to the larger culture, of course, and the way that culture determines the values of things. And since that culture is controlled by men, it naturally privileges men's needs. A recent Gallup poll of women found that eighty-five percent of women believed that what had to change in America for them to achieve full equality was men's attitudes. And can you blame them? As I've said, my whole life has in a sense been dedicated to overturning the short-sighted beliefs of what was expected of me. In my many years in construction, working always with men, I was very conscious of the fact that I would always begin from a place of not being taken seriously—and then, and only then, after I'd demonstrated my expertise ten times over, would I be accepted as an equal.

Women and Investment

Everything I've said up till now has been about the making of money by women. But what about the investing of money by women? The problem is that when it comes to investing their money, the financial cards are stacked against women. Women live longer than men and need more money to last through retirement. At the same time, they earn less. And they are more likely to take time off during their careers to care for children or parents, and to run a family, and are less likely to have pension plans. These factors, combined with more frequent job changes, mean women lose seniority and sometimes are unable to invest in pension plans.

The real tragedy here is that women are great investors. Don't take it only from me. Hard-headed professional financial analysts agree that women are more goal-driven than men. They work better in advisory relationships and are more willing to take a long-term view—all essential characteristics for investment success. So ladies, take heart!

Actually, many women today are aware of the difficulty and are determined to do something about it. A series of recent polls testify to the fact that the single overriding concern of women today is economic survival. Their families, health, and problems of time management and stress follow in close order. But economics rules the roost. Interestingly enough, this same poll had some encouraging numbers for those hoping that things were changing for the better. The poll interviewed not only mothers, but daughters and found out that for daughters, seventy percent of them found their financial situation better than the one their mother had had to confront. And eighty-five percent said there were more career opportunities than were available at their mother's time.

The situation for women, their rights and their pocketbooks, is complicated, but with some very hopeful signs on the horizon. Women *have* come a long way, baby. But there's no reason to rest on our laurels. We need another generation of strong women leaders, like that of Gloria Steinem and Company. Much, it is clear, still remains to be done.

CHAPTER

12

The Verdict

CHAPTER 12

I WAS IN BED, LATE AT NIGHT, WHEN THE PHONE RANG. It was a reporter from the *New York Daily News*, calling to offer his congratulations and ask for a comment. I was stunned. I had only found out myself moments before—how could he possibly have known so quickly?

Norman Sheresky had explained to me that I wasn't alone in waiting for the verdict, because apparently divorce lawyers were also waiting, standing on the steps of the courthouse, eager to hear the outcome of the case that was going to have a precedent-shattering impact on divorce law in America.

What I didn't know was that the media was also waiting, and that in the days after the winning verdict, all hell would break loose, with media coverage from coast to coast, endless radio and television interviews, and eventually documentaries by CBS 48 HOURS and the BBC.

It was the size of the award, it was the history-making fact of fifty percent, and it was the way in which, at a stroke, the words "homemaker" or "housewife" were suddenly and forever given a whole new meaning.

I was happy, of course. I was deeply vindicated, but because I'd expected the decision all along, I can't say I was especially surprised. More surprising was the sudden glare of media attention and bright lights. I never sought out this attention, and though I felt natural with it, it was only because I felt I had a useful story to tell. For many months I had been so involved with the preparation of this case that I hadn't given a thought to the notoriety that might ensue if I won. So when I realized that not only had I won, but that my case would be important both to women and to changing the structure of divorce laws in the country, I was slightly surprised. And of course, I was also very happy.

Particularly gratifying were the many letters that I got from unknowns. They made me feel that the case and its after effects would have a real bearing on future generations. Congratulations and letters from well-wishers poured in from all over the world. And, on the other hand, there were the so-called "friends" who never picked up the phone. Divorce, as I've said elsewhere in this book, is a social truth serum, which tends to bring out whatever's hidden in people's feelings both about you and the state of their own marriage. In this case, it provided the strange spectacle of people who didn't know me going out of their way to congratulate me, while old acquaintances sometimes pretended we had never met.

The legal decision itself obviously came out of a cultural climate that was ripe and ready for a breakthrough of this kind.

It was a victory for American women .And yet, we all know that divorce laws still trail reality by a long stretch. Marriage is an imperfect institution, and so is the procedure for ending it. I feel like my contribution was to open the door a crack—a door that had been kept closed for centuries, with the entire weight of the world sitting on it to keep it shut. That door is now ajar. There's some fresh air blowing into a formerly stuffy dark space. It will be up to the women who come after me to expand upon my work, continue the fight for their rights and justice, and open that door to the light of the future.

AFTERWORD

OPENING UP TO YOU, THE READER, HAS NOT been easy for me. By nature, I'm a private person. Whatever successes and failures I've had in my life, I've kept them to myself. But I'm sharing my candid thoughts with you in the hope that you can draw some encouragement from them.

My message in this book is simple: success is a learned habit. It's not something you're born with. It's something you acquire, through the old and often difficult method of trial and error. If your reaction to setback is: oh what a terrible thing; I'm going to shut my eyes and hope it goes away—well, it will never go away; it will fester.

You must learn through adversity; learn by looking deep into yourself to gain a clear sense of who you are, what you want, and what your motives are at bottom. Life is negotiation with issues, and there's an infinite amount of them—sentimental, economic, legal, physical. How much easier it is to move through these when you walk with the firm, sure step of the person who knows herself, who's done the work to figure out who she is. Also important to remember is that *not* acting is the worst thing of all. The anxiety that builds up around inaction is almost always worse than the result of the action taken.

I hope this book will give you enough information to stimulate your mind to the thoughts that will best benefit you. No book will give you the exact formula to resolve your issues. But disciplined thought will allow you to achieve your own point of view.

To think positive, to always have faith, to keep enough strength to dream, to aspire—this is my credo. One of my favorite dyslexics, Winston Churchill, put it nicely when he said, "We will never give up, never give up." Closer to home, my father used to end conversations with me by always saying, "Keep on fighting." I have, and I hope you will too.

— *Vira Hladun-Goldmann*

APPENDICES

In this section, I've included several chapters that might help readers widen their understanding of topics touched on in the book. There are autobiographical details, some practical, concrete advice on how best to go about obtaining a quick, fair divorce, and a selection of press coverage of the historic decision.

APPENDIX A

MY WORK LIFE

LIKE MY MOTHER, I SUPPOSE, I'VE ALWAYS WORKED hard. Ukrainian women, as I've mentioned, are tireless workers, and the trait is passed on from generation to generation. My grandmother would give birth, and then two or three days later would be back out in the fields weeding and sowing. My mother worked shoeless in the fields of Ukraine the first sixteen years of her life, and when she came to America, she broke production records at her factory. In our neighborhood, she was known as "the woman who worked." Where other mothers were often satisfied with running a home, my mother did that and also held down a full-time job. When home, with the cooking and cleaning over, she was still busy knitting or crocheting. This continued even in front of the radio, her fingers moving, the needles clicking as she listened to the news. The woman wasn't idle a single day of her life.

But it wasn't just my mother. My father was a hard worker, too—almost as hard a worker as my mother was. And there was no such thing in my childhood home as women's work and men's work. It was simply the work to be done. My father didn't think twice about putting the apron on and shaking out the mop on the front porch; my mother was deeply handy and would patch and repair at the drop of a hat. Together they moved through the day in a wordless understanding of each other's needs. Blame or responsibility was never assigned. Every thing we did, we did together. Whoever came home first started dinner. Whatever there was to be done, we did it—efficiently—and without asking first.

My first job was at age ten. I was the neighborhood personal shopper, designated by local housewives as the girl who could be trusted to take a dollar bill to the store, buy a pound of butter, and bring back the change. The dime or nickel I was paid invariably ended up—with a satisfying clink—in my sugar bowl bank.

At age thirteen I graduated to babysitting, especially for the Kingsley family next door. From fourteen on, I began working seasonally on a farm, getting up very early in the morning to be in downtown Rochester at five am. Picked up by the farmer in his truck, I would spend the day harvesting strawberries, peaches, and string beans.

Sixteen was also exciting because sixteen was the age Sibley, Lindsey and Curr, the local department store, would hire sales staff. Freshly ironed and starched, I was there the day after my sixteenth birthday. It was a real job as opposed to the small change of baby sitting that had preceded it. I was pulling down the miraculous sum of twenty-two dollars per week. I had arrived! And I could finally buy my own clothes. Not that I spent extravagantly. Anything but, in fact. My parents had instilled in me from the very first that money was not to be used for the luxuries of life. I may have dreamed of the fashionable salons of Paris, but my feet, directed by my parents, were very much on the ground.

My father exemplified this attitude to a T. He refused whenever possible to modernize, to spend money on what he regarded as articles that were useful only because they were trendy or new. This former captain of the Ukrainian Army would have things done his way, or no way at all. If that way involved not spending money, so much the better.

All of this was underlined by the keen, continual need we all felt coming from Ukraine. My mother would often say at dinner, "Babtsya (grandmother) doesn't have enough food, and neither does anyone else over there, so how could you leave that pile of peas on your plate?"

"Well then give me less, mother," I'd reply.

My parents careful, conservative attitude toward money and work has stood me in good stead in life. I learned early on that nothing in this world is handed to you on a platter. The things you desire may be approached only through hard work, and there are no short cuts or easy ways.

At college, where I majored in education and minored in art, I began working in B Forman's, an exclusive, upscale store of women's and men's apparel. This was the equivalent of Saks Fifth Avenue for Rochester. I both modeled the women's outfits and sold. And in selling I discovered gifts I hadn't known I possessed. In fact, I outsold all the other salespeople there, grew beloved of the manager, Mr. Zelder, and was promoted to be Hickock Girl. This was not exactly the White Rock Girl, but for Rochester it was pretty exciting. It meant that I worked as a hostess and sales girl in a special exhibition room, where I sold the Hickock garters, wallets, and men's accessories.

College life was meanwhile opening my eyes in a hundred ways. It was an endless round of excitement and study. My favorite classes were the psychology courses, which allowed me to analyze the wide spectrum of daily things we take for granted. To study better, I quickly worked out a system that allowed me to conquer my dyslexia. While the professor was lecturing to the class, I would take such notes as I could. Afterward, having made friends with one of the good students, I would borrow her notes, fill in what was left out, and then go home and read the notes and the homework assignment out loud. That was the key: reading out loud. If I read silently, I could have done it twenty times without getting anywhere. But in hearing the sounds out loud, I was able to identify and make sense of them in a way I never would if they remained on the quicksand of the printed page. I had moved out of the dorm into a quiet home, in part for this reason, and by bearing down with total concentration on my work, I was able to get good grades.

Education is very important to Ukrainian families, and I was an only child. It doesn't take much to guess just how proud my parents were on the day of graduation. After the ceremony, held on the main lawn of the college, my father hugged me so hard I thought he was going to break some ribs.

Upon graduating, I began teaching in a leafy little suburb of Rochester called Pittsford. From the first, I found teaching a deeply satisfying job. This satisfaction was almost entirely about watching the growth and progress of the children who would expand before my eyes. Children at that age are like sponges. They are often insecure, but they are ready to experience—often a great, hungry desire to experience and learn about their environment. Of course, they also have the attention span of gnats. But they are excited to see and do and learn. Working to overcome their individual difficulties, inspiring them while tailoring the learning rhythms to their needs— these were the challenges, and I loved them. Teaching would be a job I would do happily for seven years. It would take a major event in my life to cause me to give up a career I treasured. That event was called pregnancy.

APPENDIX B

THE NUTS AND BOLTS OF DIVORCE

Adivorce is a legal process with a specific beginning. One of you must file papers calling for a divorce. No matter how passionate you feel about the need for ending your marriage, all the talking and wishing and hand-wringing in the world won't in and of itself bring a divorce about. So you must make the move and file the papers, either with an attorney, a paralegal, or by yourself, if you've taken the time to bone up on what's required.

At this point, the bureaucratic waltz of divorce has begun. Now is the time to move as quickly and decisively as possible. If the divorce is amicable, as ours was in the larger, more important sense (we were contesting the family fortune, but doing so with dignity and affection), then you needn't take certain precautions. But many divorces aren't amicable, and in those cases, you must act to protect yourself. Temporary orders are one recourse—a recourse which often acts to prevent assets from mysteriously disappearing, or debts being mysteriously run up. Arrangements must be made for the children, if they are still at home: who will be responsible for them? Where will they reside? The family house is often a bone of contention in divorce trials. It is best to try to decide early who will be staying in the house while the divorce is settled and who will be paying the mortgage and taxes on the home. Do not, in any case, ever leave the house without first talking to the attorney. There are women who under the sway of emotion and the desire to leave an unhappy setting, have simply upped and vacated the house—with serious legal consequences down the line. Another early series of decisions arises if there is a disproportion in the income of the two spouses, in which case you have to work out the answers to questions regarding support, attorney's fees, and other expenses.

The point is that some divorces can be complex, and in such cases a variety of court orders may be necessary before trial or settlement to stabilize the situation. Acting with a certain clarity at this point can ensure a smoother transition, making it easier on both yourself and your children.

Outside Help

Fairly early on, depending on the situation, your lawyer will make a determination as to what kind of outside help to bring in. This can range the gamut from psychologists to real estate specialists, accountants or specialists in art valuation. It may be useful if you try to think before you begin if anyone with an expertise outside the strictly legal may be useful in your case. Expert appraisers are often key in fairly dividing the marital assets of couples with art or collectible holdings.

One of the most common advisors called in on divorce cases is the tax accountant. Taxes are often a quagmire for divorcing parties. There are many complex angles to tax and divorce. For example, alimony payments have tax consequences. Retaining an asset, whether the family home or a stock portfolio, brings with its specific taxable liabilities. There are assets that come with loss carryforwards already attached and some with useful deductions for income tax purposes. Assets can be taxed at lower rates than ordinary income, but they can also be taxed at a higher rate. To panic and withdraw money from pensions or IRA accounts can have tax and tax penalty consequences.

This is just the tip of the iceberg. Taxes loom on every side in a divorce. And while many family law practitioners have a passing acquaintance with the tax code, if you feel you need more expert assistance, don't hesitate to ask.

Finances

Taxes are just one corner of finances generally, of course, and finances are nothing less than the Bermuda Triangle of divorce, that space into which all sorts of good wishes, lawyers' fees and endless judicial headaches disappear. Quite often, the man has controlled what happened to the money during the marriage, and he's perfectly ready to do the same during divorce. If a woman during her marriage has been on top of the family finances, has imagined herself a real partner with her husband in the fiscal as well as the emotional aspects of marriage life, then she is probably prepared for the financial tussle of divorce. She probably has a fair sense of where the assets are, and more or less what they're worth.

If she doesn't, then she'll have to begin the laborious process of digging everything out. Remember: *this is not spying*. This is you claiming your rights on a shared investment. You should know just as much as the other person knows. You're not outside your jurisdiction. You're thoroughly within your human rights.

From a legal point of view, divorce is a kind of business transaction, and like most business transactions requires as much documentation as possible. Although your mind may not be exactly in this place at that moment in time, force yourself. The most important thing to do is make copies of everything related to financial transactions: tax returns, all insurance policies of any kind, bank statements, credit card statements, will, trusts, copyrights, patents, royalties, art or property valuations—basically, if there was any kind of document of any kind relating to finance, make sure you have a record of it.

This is not only good for bolstering your case and tracking down the true wealth of your family—the better to equitably distribute it—but it also saves you a lot of money that would otherwise be spent hiring expensive private investigators to vet your finances.

I've stressed repeatedly in this book the importance of writing The History of My Marriage. I'd now like to add a companion task: writing The History of Our Finances. Sit down in a chair, clear your mind, and write down everything you can think of with as much detail as possible about your finances, marital and personal. Make a list of every asset you and your spouse own, the date on which they were purchased or acquired, the price paid, the amount still outstanding (if any), the current value, and any arguments you can muster on who is the proper owner of this asset, you or your spouse. And do this, if possible, BEFORE the divorce has begun, BEFORE you two have turned into professional combatants, and he's had a chance, as husbands in this circumstance have been known to do, to make the documents vanish.

The more information you can bring to bear on this under your own steam, the better. Here are several things you can do which might not ordinarily occur to you but which could prove very useful at this early stage of divorce:

1. Make a list of everyone you know who could conceivably be a witness. This includes people who may deal with your children, such as doctors or guidance counselors or teachers. It may include your stockbroker or your banker. Certainly it will often include your neighbors. It might even include friends who saw the two of you under strain and would make friendly witnesses.

2. Call a realtor and quietly ask for an appointment for a valuation of your house or apartment. Make the realtor understand the need for discretion. On the heels of this valuation, copy as much information as possible to do with the mortgage. Get, if possible, a copy of the deed and one of the mortgage statement showing the payments and balance still outstanding.

3. The video camera can be a divorcing woman's best friend! Take a long, detailed, lingering video (or still camera) cruise around the house, itemizing everything, from lamps and furnishings to what's in the garage and attic. A photographic image furnishes irrefutable proof that the object was once nestling under your roof, and particularly during those months around a divorce when spouses can become a bit light-fingered with treasured personal effects, it can be quite useful.

4. Certain actions have such a ring of finality to them that women will do almost anything to avoid them. Cancelling credit cards is one of them, and yet it's among the best measures to protect herself a woman has. It is commoner than you might think for spouses before or during a divorce to rack up large credit card bills, and this can be avoided by cancelling all joint credit accounts and getting one in your name. Doing this also allows you a cushion if and when the spouse has a tantrum and abruptly cancels the cards.

5. Getting your own bank account is a related action, which can have similarly beneficial effects. If you haven't had one, your own bank account is an important declaration of independence, and also, on a practical level, allows you to deposit and withdraw monies without your spouse being aware of it (though you should remember that the court can grant him that privilege if he asks for it)

6. Bring your family (your parents and children) into the loop. The point here is that nothing is gained, once you're certain divorce is on its way, by waiting or attempting to sugarcoat the news. Better your children hear about it from you, with tenderness and compassion, than from a neighbor. If you and your spouse have worked out a joint custody plan, share it with the children as soon as possible. It's an enormous psychological relief for children to know that though their parents are splitting up, they are united in having already worked out a plan for the children's care. On the other hand, it is unhealthy for children to be privy to the actual discussions, arguments and pros and cons of divorce. They are better left out of such things, and they should never be used as mediators or go betweens either.

7. Don't necessarily hasten to file your tax returns alone. The difficulty of taxes and divorce bears repeating here. Although the advice to not file your taxes alone

may run counter to the divorcing logic of "act alone and in your own best interest at all times," the fact is it's worth your while to spend the time and expense consulting a tax attorney who should be able to tell you fairly quickly whether or not there are any financial benefits to filing together as opposed to separately.

8. Don't sign documents presented to you by your spouse without the presence and counsel of a lawyer. Many women, especially those who have not been interested in their marital finances before, have signed dozens of documents in their married life based on their husband's say-so. Stop that process as soon as there is a whiff of divorce in the air!

9. Consider upcoming medical and dental work and make your choices accordingly. Do so knowing that upon separation, your spouse may not be required to pay your medical and dental expenses, and in most states the marital estate won't have to pay them either. The truth is, you'll need all your energy and concentration for the upcoming divorce, so it would probably be best if you put off any medical procedures until afterward. But they can't always wait, of course.

10. Begin the process of drawing up your will or revising it. This will probably not be the first thing on your mind when you're contemplating divorce, but the truth is that if you die intestate (without a will) in most states, the majority of your assets will revert to your husband, even if you're in the middle of a divorce. Your will and trusts do not change automatically just because your marriage is ending. I was fortunate in consulting a crackerjack trust and estates lawyer first thing. This was useful to me and it can be useful to you too. If you do not make these decisions before divorcing, the courts will often enforce earlier agreements made in happier times. For the umpteenth time: plan ahead!

APPENDIX C

RESTORATION AND ME

SUBSTITUTE TEACHING AND TUTORING WASN'T ALL I did after giving up my regular teaching job to raise my child. All during Olexa's girlhood, whenever I had a free moment to myself, I would spend it reading up on antiques and interiors of the eighteenth and nineteenth century. I loved this rugged, colorful period of American history.

And I always felt, as I studied, that I was somehow following up on a legacy left to me by my mother. As a tailor, she had always had an eagle eye for subtle differences in texture, pattern, color, and weave in clothing, and she'd passed this on to me. My aesthetic education had begun in the fabric houses of Rochester in the 1940s, places to which my mother would take me on her buying trips, always carefully pointing out to me the difference between the lesser and higher quality silks, cottons, and wools. Until I was sixteen, she designed and made all my clothing. New outfits were sewn by her twice a year, at the opening of school, and for Easter. "OK," she'd say, as the opening of school drew nearer, "Let's go to the fabric store." Once there, we would also buy the McCall's or Simplicity or Vogue patterns to be made. She would let me choose—and needless to say, my excitement was EXTREME.

But I wasn't excited only about getting new clothes. It was also a chance to be close to my mother. In fact, given that my mother was not especially communicative, it was in areas like design, clothes and decoration that we had some of our deepest exchanges. She let me decorate my bedroom at thirteen, and—an unforgettable moment—I picked the wallpaper out. She asked for my input in decorating decisions around the house, and you can bet I took this very seriously indeed! Choosing carpets, matching fabrics to wallpaper, paint to curtains—understanding our home as a puzzle of different surfaces which must be carefully paired for best advantage gave me a visual education and a hunger for beauty that has provided much joy and pleasure in my adult life.

It will be little surprise then if I mention that I started collecting as soon as I could. Fresh out of college and essentially broke, I nonetheless toured the junk and antiques shops and began amassing a collection of antique glass, furniture and accessories—all within my budget. My first bed in NY was an antique brass model bought for the then princely sum of thirty-five dollars. When I got married, and we had no money, I went to a second hand store, Mr. Joseph's, on the 30's on the West Side, and began picking out the battered old stuff with which we furnished our tiny home. As we began to make a little bit more money, I sold these pieces and then climbed slowly up the ladder of quality, buying more valuable antiques as I went.

My goal from the start had been to collect classic American antiques. And when I could finally afford to, and had the time to, I began serious collecting. It was the combination of simple design, precious patina, and complex history that captured my imagination. Every collectible has a history, and I think that one of the benefits of being raised by immigrant parents is that you grow up with a kind of double vision that makes you historically aware. You go through your days simultaneously aware both of your present surroundings, and the other, foreign place your parents came from. If your parents are from a land which, like Ukraine, was continuously invaded over the centuries, then you have a sense of the fragility of life as well. With this as background, perhaps it's easier to understand how, when I saw eighteenth-century pieces made by recent immigrants to America, (because, at that time, everybody was a recent immigrant to America) I was immediately intrigued.

The history of eighteenth and nineteenth-century American furniture and decorative arts is taken from England, and from the British master craftsmen who immigrated to the states. Once here, they settled mainly in New England, where they began making furniture using American hardwoods like maple and cherry and giving a new fineness and delicacy to the traditional lines. To my eye there is an elegance to antiques of the eighteenth and nineteenth-century American northeast that is unparalleled.

Over time, as an offshoot of my work with furniture, I fell in love with the school of naïve American painting of the early-nineteenth century. From the start I was drawn to the simplicity and freshness of these unschooled artists who worked in small towns in upstate New York and New England. Many of them were "limners," itinerant painters who supported themselves daubing family portraits and homey little scenes of daily life and worked with cheerful indifference to the great Italian and French masters. My criterion for buying was a simple one: do I want to live with this in my private life? For these naïve or "folk" art painters of the early American period, the answer was an easy yes for the best of reasons: in their candor, freedom and complete lack of pretension, I saw myself!

From here, it was only a matter of time before I began a career as a restorer of eighteenth and nineteenth-century structures and interiors. I've restored nine period homes and learned a lot about people, materials, and the eccentricities of old domestic structures while doing so. The challenge in restoration, working with period structures, is to do the research, master the facts, and then meticulously restore them to their original eighteenth-century splendor, while unobtrusively incorporating twentieth-century conveniences.

These projects, I should add, were done on the side of my marriage and home life, and I never allowed them to interfere. Houses were not part of Robert's responsibility. They simply weren't on his horizon in life. He was looking for peace and quiet when he got back from the office, and that was about it. Not to say he didn't appreciate what I did. He liked living in homes which were, as he put it, "living museums." But the world of period restoration was my world.

Each house taught me something different, as I say. I did tons of my own studying before touching a single brick on a facade. I combed books and town records, burrowed through libraries, and eventually amassed a fair historical library of my own. I would go to museums in the area too. It was important not to get only the architectural particulars, but the flavor of the people who lived there. One of the many difficulties in restoring homes in the era before mass production is that a lot of details are one of a kind. The staircases of the houses, for example, were often custom made, with all sorts of particular details that gave me a devil of a headache to reproduce. Over time, I traveled to most of the famous historical homes in the Northeast and in Colonial Williamsburg as well.

I look back on those period renovations of mine with a great sense of satisfaction—but that isn't to shortchange the way I had to struggle, on a near daily basis, with the ingrained attitudes of men taking orders on a construction site from a woman. I started out doing this in the '70s, remember, and construction people, bless their hearts, were never exactly in the vanguard of women's lib. I didn't ask for special treatment, I wanted only basic cooperation, and that they deal with me as they would any other client. And therein lay the problem. It was a genuinely difficult day-to-day struggle, particularly at the beginning, when it seemed I was taken advantage of by nearly every contractor I worked with, and I myself was under serious financial constraints and had to stretch every dollar as far as it would go. But tenacity, as I've said, is one of my main gifts, and I learned on the job. I also benefited, eventually, from the arrival of one of the many angels in my life who have shown up at difficult intervals to help me out. The angel in this case was, of all people, a German gardener and jack-of-all-trades who was without the chauvinism of his American counterparts and showed me in great detail many of the secrets of the building trade.

Restoration was and is my culminating career—a career in which all my talents and my drives have come together. In addition to the difficulty of it, the work has produced some of the deepest satisfactions of my life.

APPENDIX D

PROBLEM SOLVING

I HAVE BEEN SUCCESSFUL AS A BUSINESSWOMAN (I entered the divorce having earned eight million dollars of my own in the renovation and restoration business). During that time, I have learned much about people. Anyone who is successful in business has to have a psychological sense, and if I say so myself, I have a pretty good one. I know when someone is taking me seriously and when someone is pretending to. I know, usually, when I'm in the presence of a loafer, and when I'm in the presence of someone who is motivated to do a good job.

Restoring period homes, as I've mentioned, is a time-consuming job, full of tiny details and exacting tolerances. In addition, it's the kind of job that requires you to be able to balance the needs of all sorts of different people. It's not like an assembly line job, where you merely have to oversee the running of a machine.

And it's not like building tract houses, either. No, each job has entirely different requirements. Each job must be carefully studied and planned to the nth degree. And though, over time, you may eventually develop a crew or core group of people with whom you work well, you still have to be flexible, adaptable, and always able to anticipate the hundred new difficulties that are sure, like crabgrass, to pop up in the middle of your project.

My business principles are simple. I'm a perfectionist on the one hand, and I'm ruthlessly honest on the other—maybe even blunt at times. You have to be when you're working with people. They've got to know exactly what you expect from them. And what you expect from them, of course, is their very best. I've come across lots of bad apples in my time, yet that hasn't changed my essential working method: I begin by assuming the positive about anyone I hire. I give them the benefit of the doubt from the beginning. I assume that if they have bad habits they can unlearn them. If they don't, I tell them to take their hat and scram.

It's hard enough for men to accept a woman as boss. What's really hard for them sometimes is to accept not only that I'm their superior, but that I know as much about their job as they do. When I was building the fifth floor of my townhouse, the main mason, a Uruguayan gent who was very good at what he did, had a problem with taking instruction from me at the beginning. He had started building a brick wall, and I explained that the joints or spaces between the bricks were too wide, and they would have to be adjusted. This is not acceptable, I explained to him. He was perfectly polite but did nothing about it. I then called up his boss and said, "your man is doing sloppy work, and I won't stand for it." The boss told him,

"Do it. Whatever she says is the way you have to do it.." He had to remove three courses of bricks forty-feet long, so he wasn't happy! And he did it wrong again the second time. And then he did it wrong the third time. Talk about pig-headed! This man seemed to have a shape in his brain and be only able to see that one way of doing things. Finally his boss showed up personally and chewed him out. Look Sam, I told the mason, you're going to be working with me, and you're going to have to get used to that. He answered by saying, I'm sorry, but the problem is I'm not used to taking instruction from women, I'm used to working with men. Well, I told him, that's not the way it's going to be around here. But if it makes you feel any better, I'll make sure I wear pants around the house every day. This way you can keep saying to yourself, she's really a man! And then we'll get along fine. He laughed, we made up, and we worked magnificently well together.

You must, in this life, be able to cut through the baloney and get to the crux of the matter. It's too easy to get caught up in surface impressions. You have to clearly see your goal and then know how to put closure on, how to seal a deal. Divorce certainly was the classic example of that in my life. Realizing that the marriage had become irreversibly stagnant, I decided to put an end to it, and that was that.

In addition to knowing how to achieve closure, and how to make your expectations clear to your co-workers, you must be deeply organized. A job like renovating period homes, as I say, is an endless rain of tiny details, and the only way to keep the work running smoothly is to be there 100 percent, body and soul, and know where every screw, bolt and plank must go BEFORE they've actually gotten there, on-site.

It all gets back to problem solving. Problem solving is half of life, and never more so than in the world of business. My education in problem solving goes all the way back to my earliest conversations with my father, when he would help me methodically open up and discuss whatever it was that was bothering me. Later in life, I recall that I was practice teaching in a kindergarten in Brighton, New York. The teacher I was substituting for told me things I've never forgotten. She said, the way you get rid of problems as a teacher is by studying the situation so clearly that you eliminate them before they even crop up. It's like a game of chess. When you play chess well, you look five or six moves ahead. When you know how to problem solve, you see that extra inch into the future so that you've already got an answer ready when the problem presents itself. Problems will be coming at you your whole life long; you have to develop tools to resolve them. Solve one, and there's another waiting around the corner. The quicker you move through them, the less you'll have waiting for you, slowing you down.

Teaching, as I say, presented hundreds of tiny difficulties. Take the way I helped my kindergartners through the long, cold Rochester winters. Typically they would come in frozen from top to bottom and looking like icicles. They had particular problems putting their feet in their boots. Try as they might, they seemed unable to master the task and would always get their feet stuck halfway in. I still remember the yowls of frustration that would arise in the classroom. You can explain to them what to do, but an excited five-year- old has a limited attention span. *Clearly*, some showing was in order. What to do? I brought in a box of plastic bags, which they put over their shoes, and then slipped them easily into their boots.

Voila! Problem solved. The same kids were also having trouble figuring out how to put on their coats. Believe it or not, at age five, the "what sleeve first" decision is a big and often frustrating one. After thinking about it, I came up with a neat solution. I had the kids lay the coat down on the floor, first. Then each of them stepped on the shoulders of the coat, picked up the right sleeve, and then left sleeves, and then tipped the coat up in the air over their heads. I still remembered the satisfied smiles on the little faces. The school bus would be waiting outside, its exhaust puffing in the winter air. They would line up, proudly give me an individual hug and kiss, and it was good bye till tomorrow. They were terrific, my kids!

These examples, as modest as they may be, stay with you forever. And though the kinds of problems you end up solving in business situations eventually become much more complex, the same principles of anticipation, clarity and generosity abide.

APPENDIX E

PRESS COVERAGE
OF THE HISTORIC EVENT

AMERICAN PRESS COVERAGE

•*New York Daily News*, April 23, 1998

A Sutton Place "housewife" yesterday won a whopping forty-three million dollar divorce settlement—the largest equitable distribution award in N.Y. State history. Vira Hladun-Goldman, sixty-three, stunned her husband, a New York banker, by walking away from a three-decade marriage with exactly fifty percent of the couple's eighty-six million dollar fortune..."It's a fair ruling," said a victorious Vira Goldman after hearing the news. "Nobody does it alone. He had a great partner taking care of him."

•*New York Times*, April 23, 1998

"Notwithstanding their substantial wealth," Justice Tolub wrote in his eleven-page decision, "Mrs. Goldman continued to cook

Mr. Goldman's meals and she gave him haircuts throughout their marriage, even up until their separation in 1996. Given the value of the nonremunerated services, Mrs. Goldman as spouse, homemaker for thirty-three years, mother and life partner who aided and facilitated in the appreciation of the marital property, is entitled to an award of fifty percent."

•*Business Week*, August 3, 1998
In the past, settlements involving the superrich generally favored the spouse earning more money. That was usually the husband, who could usually count on keeping at least two thirds of the couple's joint assets, and sometimes more. But in a stunning April twenty second decision, Tolub ruled that Hladun-Goldman (as she is now known) was entitled to fifty percent of the pie, including forty-four million in restricted Congress stock that the company was obliged to buy back. It was the largest courtroom divorce award in New York State history. "In a long-term marriage, "Tolub decreed, "the distribution of property should be equal or as close to equal as possible."

•*The Wall Street Journal*, April 23, 1998
The judge wrote, "If Mr. Goldman was the guiding force behind Congress, then it is also clear Vira Goldman was an equal partner."

New York attorney Norman Sheresky, who represents Mrs. Goldmann, applauded the decision. "While equitable doesn't always mean equal, Mrs. Goldman was entitled to fifty percent."

•*New York Law Journal*, April 23, 1998
In making the award, Judge Walter B. Tolub... cited Mrs.

Goldman's substantial contribution as a homemaker to the marriage. She raised their child, who is now grown, without help, entertained without a full-time maid until 1986, and gave Mr. Goldman haircuts until they separated in 1996. Justice Tolub wrote, "Mrs. Goldman was involved in every phase of Mr. Goldman's existence."

•*ABA Law Journal*, November 1998
Goldman accomplished what she set out to do (In the process she)...reshaped views about the ways judges determine awards in high-asset divorces involving long-term marriages.

The concept of "marital partnership," previously recognized only in community property states, is gaining ground as a legal term in equitable distribution states as well. Courts are being forced to justify unwritten rules that place arbitrary caps on the amount non-working spouses can collect in high-asset cases. And judges are being asked to consider whether gender bias contributes to the way they value the contributions of wealthy but nonwage-earning wives.

Perhaps more significant, by refusing to settle out of court, the usual path in big-money divorce cases...Goldman has removed the stigma once associated with women who refuse to accept a comfortable settlement and leave quietly after decades of marriage. Increasingly, more women are choosing to fight rather than settle for less than half.

BRITISH PRESS COVERAGE
•*The Evening Standard*
A New York judge has broken records by awarding the wife of a bank chief a thirty-six-million-pound divorce settle-

ment. The lawyer acting for Vira Goldman said of the judgement against Core States Bank Chairman Robert Goldman, "It is not only the largest divorce settlement in an equitable distribution in the country but the largest claim tried until now in this state."

•*Sunday Times*
In contrast (to the other divorcing women in the BBC documentary) Vira parted on friendly terms with her husband and received forty-four million dollars when he died two months after their divorce. Vivacious, contentedly single and clearly the programme's heroine, she vows that her goal is to "die broke."